FOLD-AND-FLY
Paper Airplanes

Franco Pavarin & Luciano Spaggiari

Sterling Publishing Co., Inc.
New York

Photography: Mario Matteucci
Translation: Chiara Tarsia
Typesetting: G&G Computer Graphics

Library of Congress Cataloging-in-Publication Data

Pavarin, Franco
  [Aerei e navi di carta. English]
  Fold-and-fly paper airplanes / Franco Pavarin & Luciano Spaggiari.
    p. cm.
  Includes index.
  ISBN 0-8069-4257-6
  1. Paper airplanes. I. Spaggiari, Luciano. II. Title.
TL778.P38 1998
745.592—dc21   98–18288
                                                                  CIP

            1   3   5   7   9   10   8   6   4   2

Published by Sterling Publishing Company, Inc.
387 Park Avenue South, New York, N.Y. 10016
Excerpted from *Aerei e Navi di Carta*
Originally published in Italy and © 1996 by RCS Libri & Grandi Opere S.p.a., Milan
English translation © 1998 by Sterling Publishing
Distributed in Canada by Sterling Publishing
℅ Canadian Manda Group, One Atlantic Avenue, Suite 105
Toronto, Ontario, Canada M6K 3E7
Distributed in Great Britain and Europe by Cassell PLC
Wellington House, 125 Strand, London WC2R 0BB, England
Distributed in Australia by Capricorn Link (Australia) Pty Ltd.
P.O. Box 6651, Baulkham Hills, Business Centre, NSW 2153, Australia

Printed in China
All rights reserved

Sterling ISBN 0-8069-4257-6 Trade
          0-8069-4836-1 Paper

Contents

Preface

Origami is the ancient Japanese art of folding paper to create flowers, butterflies, and numerous other objects.

We believe this art originated during the early Heian era, from 737 to 806. Around the year 700, the Japanese used a small wood and paper airplane in battle. It had a sharp, pointed blade on its nose. For centuries, the Japanese have continued discover various types of folds. By building on each invention, they continued to improve. Now, they have achieved a dominant position in the world.

What happens when Western ideas unite with Japanese or Oriental arts? We experience a creative explosion. Just think of the kite. It was common all over the Orient. In the West, people discovered the kite and then forgot about it. This cycle continued until people saw that it had possibilities far beyond that of a plaything. This was the reason they worked to improve ets efficiency, staying power, and flight capacity.

The kite carried scientific instruments to new heights. Lawrence Hargrave invented a box kite, anticipating the structures used to test the first airplanes. Benjamin Franklin used a kite for his famous experiments on electricity. Franco Pavarin is to origami what Hargrave and Benjamin Franklin were tohe kite.

We owe both this and the previous books toavarin's creative mind. We also owe him thanks for many ingenious folds, creating an endless variety of shapes. The square was always the basis of origami, but for Pavarin the right form is the simplest one for his readers. Today, the standard 8 1/2 x 11 format; tomorrow, maybe six-sided, circular, or elliptical.

Franco creates airplanes with fantastic flight capacities. In his hands, paper changes its identity and seems toxceed its natural limits. In addition, he has given us container boxes, jumping frogs, and so on. In short, never lend Pavarin a newspaper, or he'll give it back to you folded in such an extraordinary way that you won't want to unfold i to read it. If you want the news, you'll just have too out and buy another newspaper.

Luciano Spaggiari

Introduction

*E*ver since I started using origami as a way to express my artistic ideas, my primary objective has been to construct paper airplanes.

My first book was about models made from square paper. It was quite successful and is now in its third edition.

I published other books on origami, and I have applied what I've learned from origami to paper airplanes. As I learned more about folding paper, I was able to create whatever models my imagination dreamed up.

In writing this book, I had the wonderful advice of my friend Spaggiari, who tested the models and informed me of his opinions.

The models belong to two groups: simple models for beginners and more complex ones for experts.

You'll find the ones for beginners on pages 14, 18, 21 and 36. They are easy to make using normal 8 1/2 x 11 paper. These models fly well even if made by beginners. I've included the first model just for fun. It is simple and quick to make, and it doesn't need glue or stapling. It flies far and even survives collision. Furthermore, it isn't dangerous because its nose is flat. It is also suitable for propulsion with a rubber band.

You'll build the other models in different ways, some with more difficult folds, but the emphasis is always on the ability to fly rather than on the resemblance to real planes.

You won't need to use glue, scissors, or a stapler.

I would like to thank Luciano Spaggiari for his collaboration, and I wish you all success and an imaginary bon voyage!

Franco Pavarin

Paper airplane competitions

Scientific American organized "The First International Paper Airplane Competition" in 1966. The competition attracted 11,851 models from 28 different countries. It also attracted letters, comments, and scientific papers. Pretty soon Leonardo da Vinci's name became linked to the competition. Many people tried to send their studies and projects to him for an opinion. Someone began spreading the rumor that Leonardo was the patron saint of the contest. They forgot that Leonardo has been dead for several hundred years! The competition became one big party, and competitors and spectators enjoyed themselves immensely.

The competition also provided an opportunity for establishing some ground rules. Two divisions were created: professional and beginner. In addition, four categories were set up: duration, distance, acrobatics, and origami.

The great number of participants created difficulties, and it was apparent that the competition needed some form of preliminary selection. Despite the extra effort involved, people never lost their sense of humor. They always managed to keep a balance between the serious and the silly. People became involved in long debates. Could they consider a vertical fall to be a flight? Could a baseball be a paper plane if it was made of paper? And so on and so forth, laughing and joking. On February 14, 1967, the 43 finalists competed in the N.Y. Hall of Science. The atmosphere was charged with enthusiasm and with atmospheric turbulence from the upward currents of the TV spotlights.

After the competition, a book was published which showed the best models.

The *Scientific American* competition triggered a chain reaction of similar competitions all over the world. I organized some, and it was during these competitions that I identified another category, duration + distance, for models that combine these two characteristics.

In 1984, another American magazine, *Science 86*, together with the Seattle Flight Museum, launched "The Second Great International Paper Airplane Contest."

If Leonardo had been the guiding light for the first competition, then compound, a multilayered composite material, was the symbol of the second.

Thus, rules for this competition promoted models constructed with multilayered paper. The competition introduced a few noteworthy categories: the under sixteens and the minimum performance, 15 ft. (4.5 m) and at least 3 seconds of flight.

More than 4,300 people from 21 different countries competed. The finals took place in Seattle on May 24, 1985. A book showing the construction diagrams of the winning models was published. In addition to these competitions, many others have helped to arouse great interest all over the world.

A typical example is the target-shooting contest which takes place every year in Seattle. Of course, the rules are modified each time. Today there are rules, regulations, and ideas for organizing different competitions. More and more people enjoy making paper airplanes and watching them fly.

The categories

Duration: Measured by rounding to a hundredth of a second. The time starts when the model leaves the launcher's hand and ends when it touches the ground.

Distance: Measured from where the model is launched to where it lands, rounding off to a sixteenth of an inch (1.5 mm). Decide beforehand whether to include the length of the model. Generally, this is not included.

Duration + distance: After measuring the time and distance as mentioned above, add the values together: seconds plus feet (m).

Acrobatics: Total the number of acrobatics and the different types of acrobatic figures. Then, evaluate the quality of the flight from 1 to 10 and add that in. (This evaluation helps counter a high number of acrobatic figures due to instability rather than maneuverability.) You may also add in the flight time, but it usually doesn't change the results. However, it may be useful in case of a draw.

Aesthetics/Origami: The participants should decide on the criteria ahead of time, but we recommend that you use a minimum flight performance.

Target-shooting: The model must land in a container. The competition may involve more than one launch to eliminate unsuccessful models. Increase the distance with each new launch. You may also establish a time limit. The winner is the participant who manages to place the greatest number of models in the container.

Multitarget-shooting: Draw a number of concentric circles on the ground and assign a point to each. Establish a launching area.
The participants launch their models for a fixed length of time or a specific number of models. At the end, add up the score of each participant's models. Before the competition, be sure to decide how to count models that land on the lines.

Run: On a defined course, such as a track, the participants launch their models individually or in "relays" and try to cross the finish line with the fewest number of throws. If a model lands off the track, the throw counts but must be repeated.

Any other idea, as long as it is amusing.

To make things easier for those of you who would like to organize airplane competitions, we have included suggested rules which you may distribute to the participants and the spectators. You may also use them to promote the competition.

Suggested rules

Paper airplane competition

Place . . . . date . . . . hour . . . .

Registration from . . . . to . . . . at . . . . time . . . .

Categories:

✔ (a)Flight duration ✔ (b)Distance ✔ (c)Acrobatics ✔ (d)Origami

Prizes:

First place per category ....

Second place per category ....

Third place per category ....

Rules:

- No participant may register more than three models per category.
- The models must be made entirely of paper (of any type and weight).
- The models must not exceed a maximum of 1 foot (30 cm).
- The models must be launched manually by the participants or, on request, by a member of the jury.
- Each participant may have two test throws per model.
- The models must be made without the aid of staplers, glue, tape, hooks, etc.

- For Category A models, the jury will measure the flight duration by measuring the amount of time the plane remains in the air.
- For Category B models, the jury will measure the distance covered by measuring the space between the edge of the launching platform and the most advanced part of the model.

- For Category C models, the jury will base its decision on the acrobatic evolutions performed by the model.
- For the Category D models, the jury will base its decision on the originality and quality of the model.
- Except for entries in Category D, the models do not have to be original.

- All models used in the competition become the property of the organizing committee.

Launching with a Rubber Band

*T*o launch a paper model with a rubber band, use a pair of scissors to cut a small notch on the fuselage. This is a simple technique, and you only need to study the diagram to understand how to do it.

The main advantage of using a rubber band to launch is the possibility of a strong, straight line thrust. This avoids the transverse force which a strong hand launch involuntarily produces. To understand just how much a hand throw influences flight instability, launch one model with your right hand and then one with your left hand. In many cases, by changing hands you remove the tendency to turn. This happens because, given its particular conformation, the human shoulder-arm-hand system allows a straight line throw only with circular movements of the joints. Thus, it is perfectly normal for a model to show some circular movement, especially with a strong launch.

With a rubber band, you'll have an easier time producing a straight line thrust. Actually, you'll have a hard time doing anything else.

Naturally, you'll have the best results from this launching technique with models that can tolerate a very strong throw. The model needs to be structurally sound (won't open up or crumple) and aerodynamically sound (doesn't tend to turn or to nose up).

Furthermore, because of the high speed involved, collisions are real crashes. In general, therefore, in order to use this technique, you'll need to:

• choose closed models
• choose models suitable for fast flight
• balance the models for straight-line flight
• make the notch and choose the point you grasp in an area where there is structural continuity without folds which could open up
• check and restore the model after each launch
• launch far from people, animals, and fragile objects.

The parts of a paper airplane

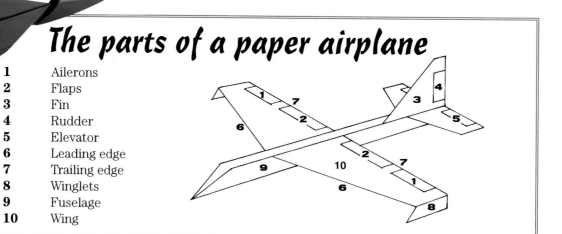

1	Ailerons
2	Flaps
3	Fin
4	Rudder
5	Elevator
6	Leading edge
7	Trailing edge
8	Winglets
9	Fuselage
10	Wing

Flight terminology and structure

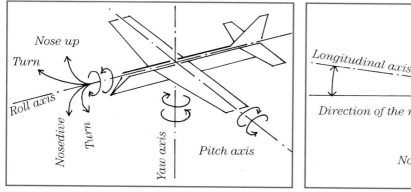

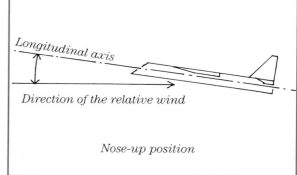

Nose-up position

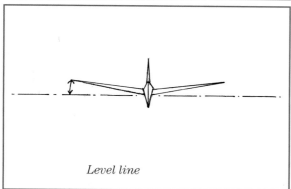

Level line

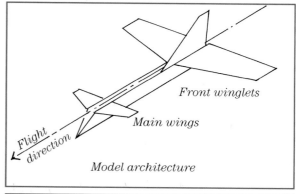

Model architecture

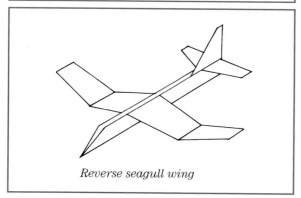

Reverse seagull wing

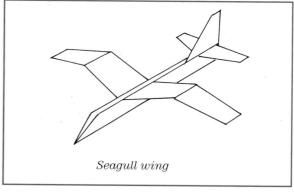

Seagull wing

Aeronautical terms

ADJUSTING: experimenting with the correct different parts of the plane and the ballast in order to allow it to fly properly.

ATTITUDE: the roll, pitch, and yaw of an aircraft while it is flying; also the direction it is pointing in relation to the horizon.

AXIS: an airplane has three axes around which it can rotate:

Rolling axis: the rotation along the longitudinal axis which causes the tips of the wings to rise and fall.

Yaw axis: the rotation which causes the nose of the plane to go to the right or to the left.

Pitch axis: the rotation which causes the nose of the plane to go up or down.

FLUTTER: a potentially dangerous movement of an aircraft caused by the interaction of aerodynamic forces and the structure of the plane. In real airplanes, this phenomenon brings about rapid structural collapse. Flags fluttering in the wind show this same reaction.

GLIDE: a flight without a motor. In our case, a glide occurs when the initial thrust diminishes and the paper airplane achieves a balance between its own aerodynamic forces and its weight.

LANDING: bringing an aircraft down to earth after a flight.

LEVEL FLIGHT: a flight with no attitude. The roll axis and the wind direction are parallel, and the wings remain level.

Nose up: a flight problem in which the plane flies upwards instead of flying on a flat line. A *nosedive* is a flight problem in the opposite direction, that is, the plane heads downwards.

STALL: a situation that occurs when the angle of attack, the angle at which the wing moves through the air, is too great and the plane loses lift. When this happens, the airplane becomes unstable and crashes.

Takeoff: the process of launching an aircraft airborne.

TURN: a problem in which the plane goes to the left or right instead of straight ahead.

UPSIDE-DOWN FLIGHT: a flight in which the plane flies upside down. In our case, the flight occurs with the paper model rotated 180°.

WARP: to curve or twist an aircraft wing in order to control the flight.

ZOOM: to cause an aircraft to climb briefly at an unusually steep angle.

Folding Symbols

- - - - -	Valley fold
-·-·-·-	Mountain fold
⌒→	Fold rotating forward
⌒→	Fold rotating backwards
⌒←	Fold forward and then back to initial position
⌒←	Fold backwards and then back to initial position
⟲→	Reverse
(↻)	Rotate 180°
⟋	Valleys fold and fold in half
⌒∣⌒	Division in two equal parts

How to fold
Initial drawing, movement, and end result

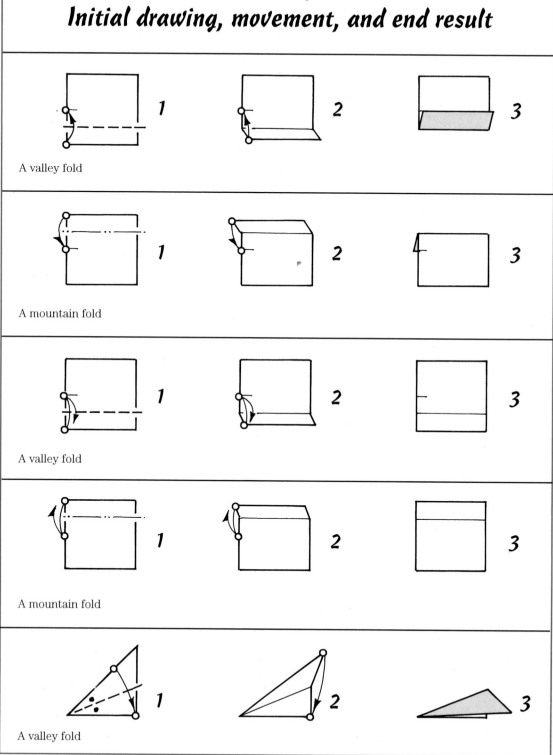

A valley fold

A mountain fold

A valley fold

A mountain fold

A valley fold

How to create turn-back folds

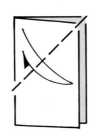

1

Make an inward
turn-back fold

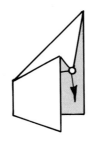

2

Make a valley fold

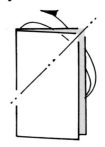

3

Remake a mountain
fold

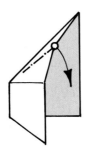

4

Open and turn
the fold back

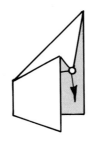

5

Insert the top point
inward and close

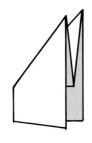

6

A completed inward
turn-back fold

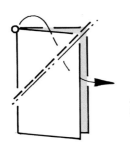

1

Make an outward
turn-back fold

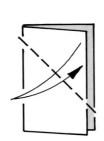

2

Make a valley fold

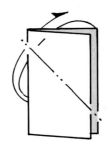

3

Remake a mountain
fold

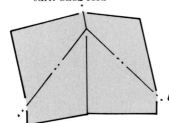

4

Open and turn the
fold back

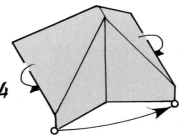

5

Reclose

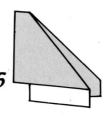

6

A completed outward
turn-back fold

Reconnaissance aircraft

A model for the distance category

Type of paper:	extra strong
Level:	very easy
Launch:	slow, accompanied
Flight path:	straight line
Behavior:	level flight
Stability:	good

*T*his is an extraordinary model because of its flying ability and ease of construction. It has a slight tendency to nose-dive, but a pair of flaps on the trailing edge will correct this defect. You may make it larger or smaller to scale without interfering with its ability to fly.

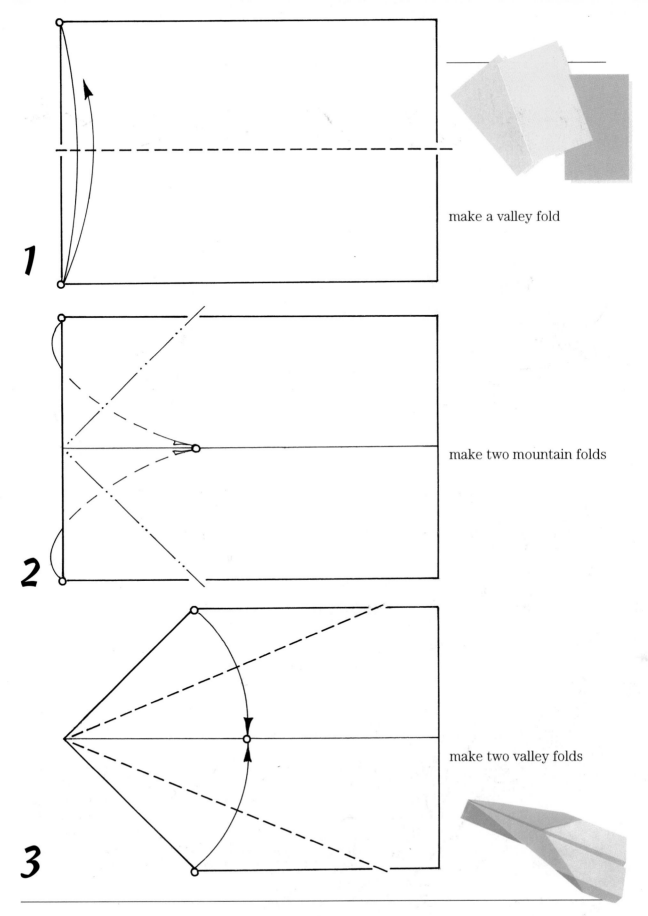

1   make a valley fold

2   make two mountain folds

3   make two valley folds

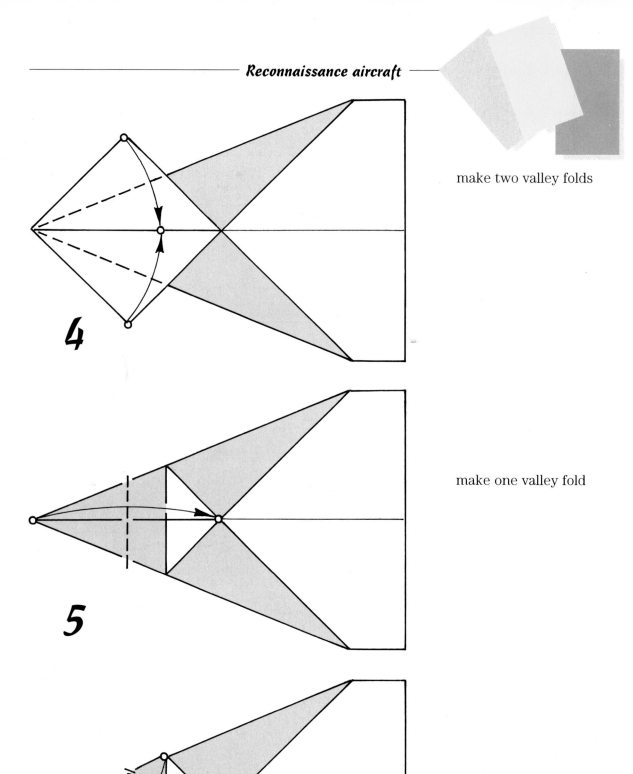

make two valley folds

4

make one valley fold

5

make two valley folds

6

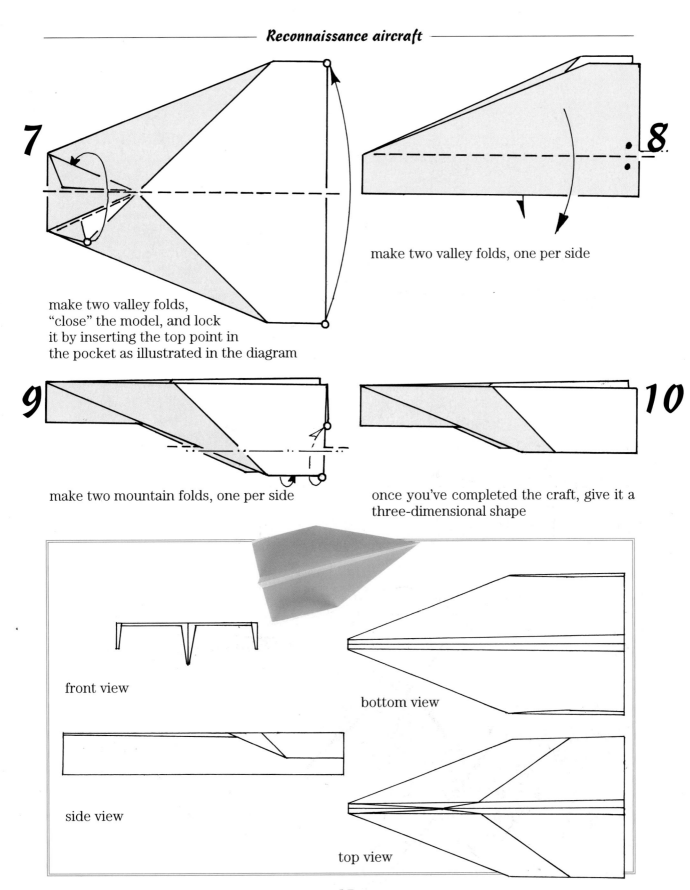

7 make two valley folds, "close" the model, and lock it by inserting the top point in the pocket as illustrated in the diagram

8 make two valley folds, one per side

9 make two mountain folds, one per side

10 once you've completed the craft, give it a three-dimensional shape

front view

side view

bottom view

top view

Rocket

A model for the duration category

Type of paper:	extra strong
Level:	very easy
Launch:	slow to medium
Flight path:	straight line
Behavior:	level flight
Stability:	good

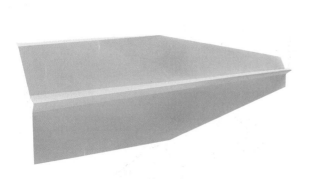

*T*his model is similar to the previous one because of its excellent flying ability and its ease of construction. In this case, we recommend you unfold a pair of flaps to correct its slight tendency to nose-dive and veer. You may also fold the winglets downwards, improving the rolling movement.

You may reduce the scale without affecting performance, except that the flight will be faster.

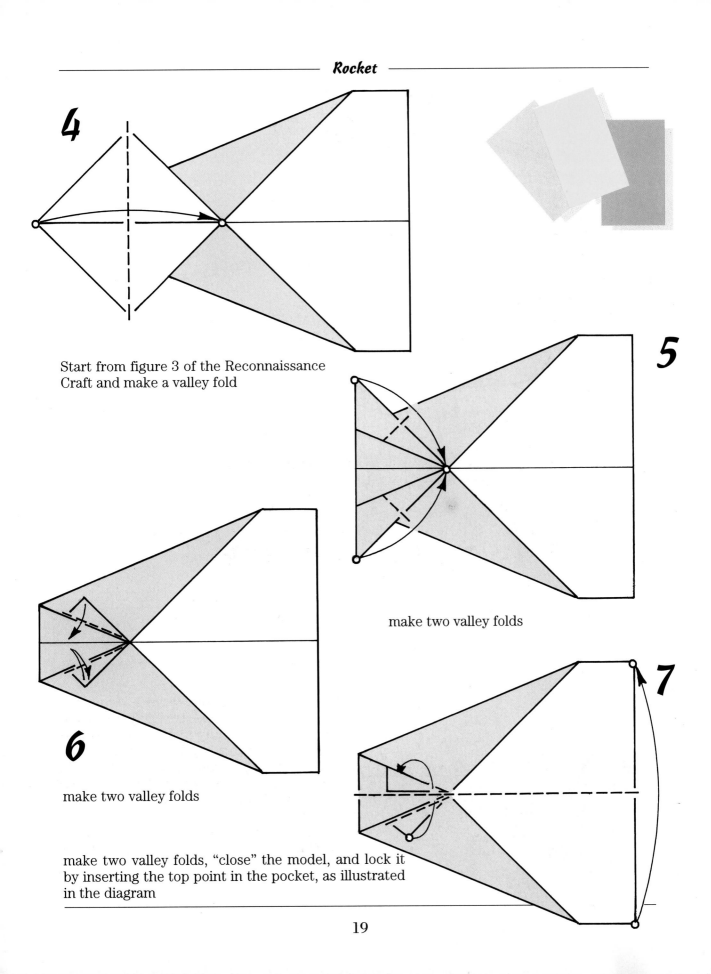

4

Start from figure 3 of the Reconnaissance Craft and make a valley fold

5

make two valley folds

6

make two valley folds

make two valley folds, "close" the model, and lock it by inserting the top point in the pocket, as illustrated in the diagram

7

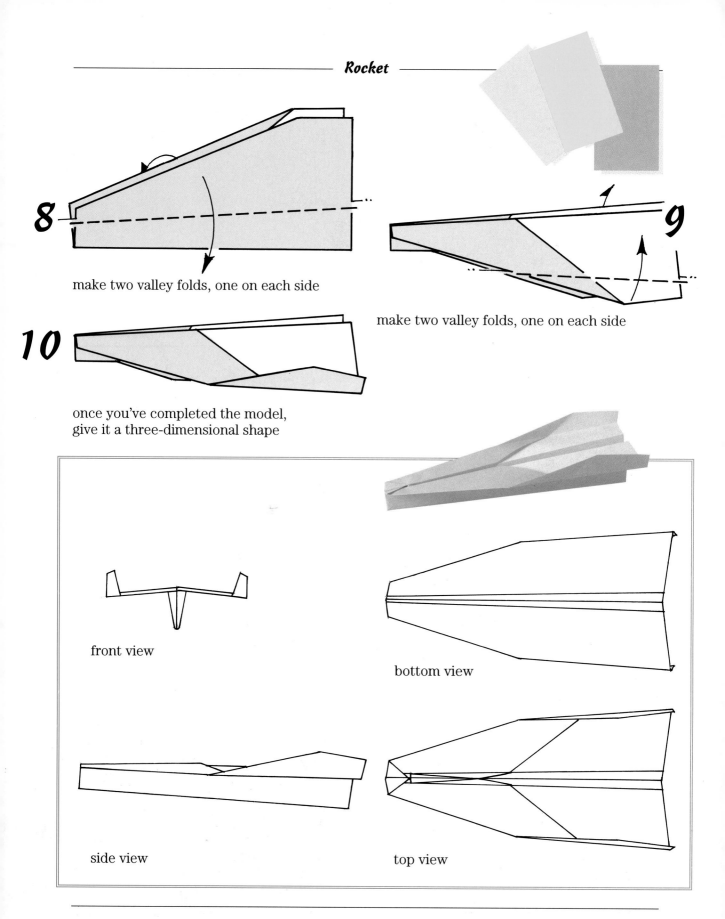

8 make two valley folds, one on each side

9 make two valley folds, one on each side

10 once you've completed the model,
give it a three-dimensional shape

front view

bottom view

side view

top view

Alien spaceship "KIR-Z"

A model for the duration category

Type of paper:	extra strong
Level:	very easy
Launch:	slow to medium
Flight path:	straight line
Behavior:	level flight
Stability:	good

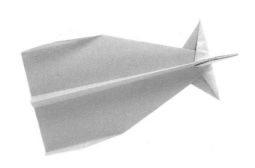

*T*his model uses the same construction design as the previous one. It has the same wing surface and is similar in weight distribution. As a consequence, it has the same slight tendency to nose drive. You may correct this defect by unfolding two small flaps on the trailing edge of the main wing. You may also try to warp the front winglet; however, this is more difficult to do and provides no particular advantage.

4

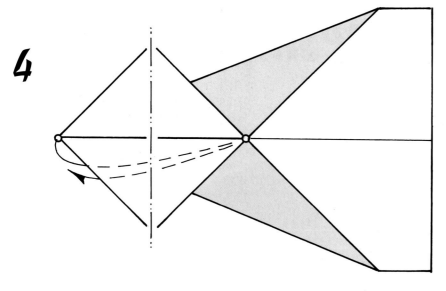

start from figure 3 of the Reconnaissance Craft and make a mountain fold and reverse

5

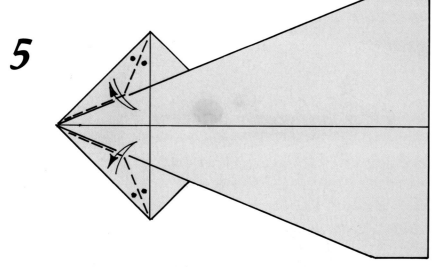

make four valley folds

6

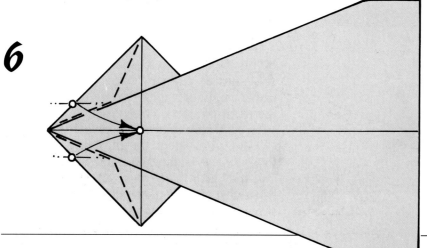

make two mountain folds and rotate, using the four valley folds created in the previous step

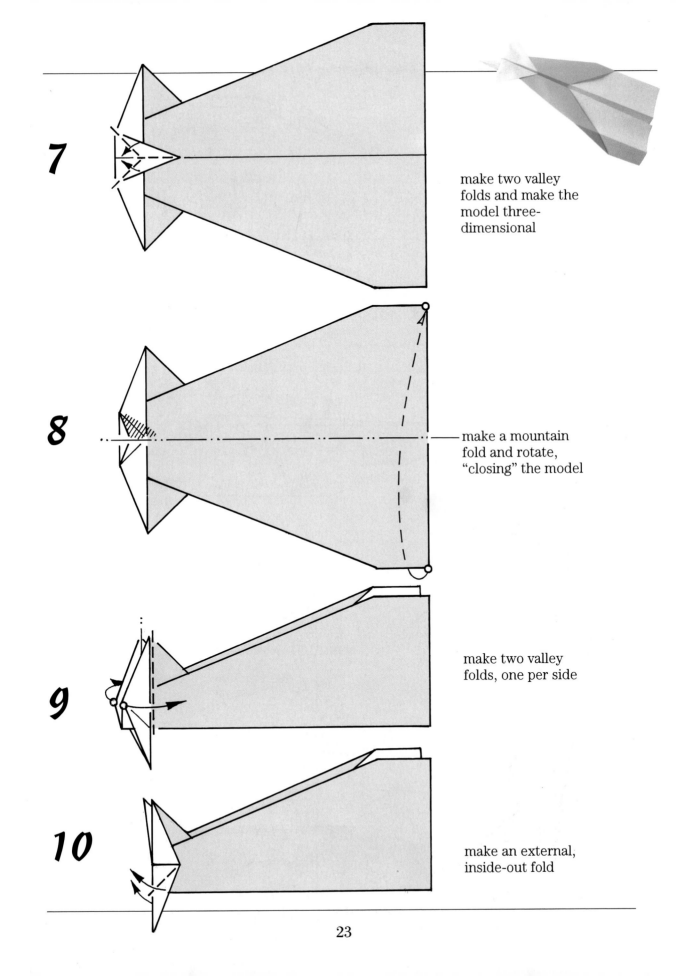

7 make two valley folds and make the model three-dimensional

8 make a mountain fold and rotate, "closing" the model

9 make two valley folds, one per side

10 make an external, inside-out fold

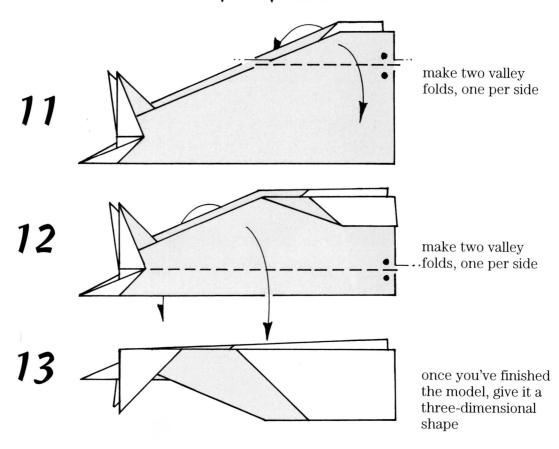

11 make two valley folds, one per side

12 make two valley folds, one per side

13 once you've finished the model, give it a three-dimensional shape

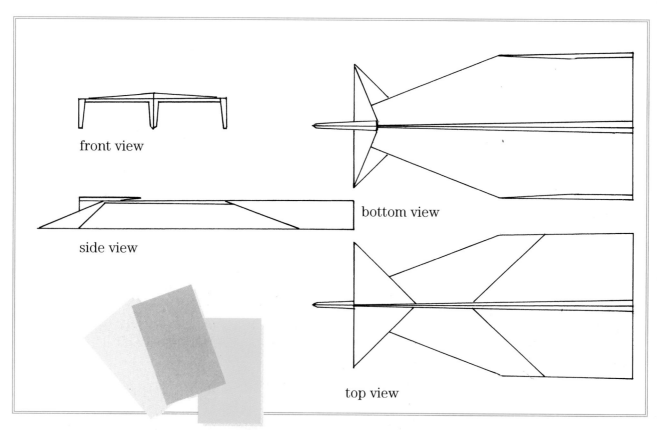

front view

side view

bottom view

top view

Extra-light two-seater Plane

A model for the distance category

Type of paper:	extra strong
Level:	intermediate
Launch:	medium to strong
Flight path:	straight line, fast
Behavior:	level flight
Stability:	excellent

*U*nlike the previous model, this superb model does not tend to nose-dive. In addition, it easily overcomes slight construction inaccuracies.

The construction steps are a little difficult, but by following the instructions carefully, the model appears almost to make itself. Launch it with a decided flick of the wrist, and you'll be amazed at how well it flies.

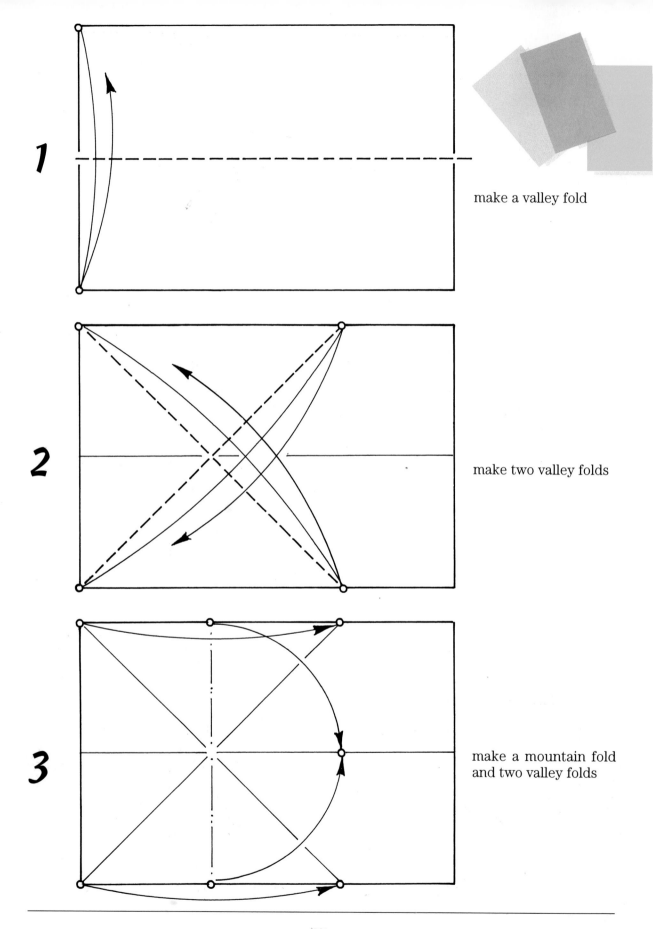

1 make a valley fold

2 make two valley folds

3 make a mountain fold
and two valley folds

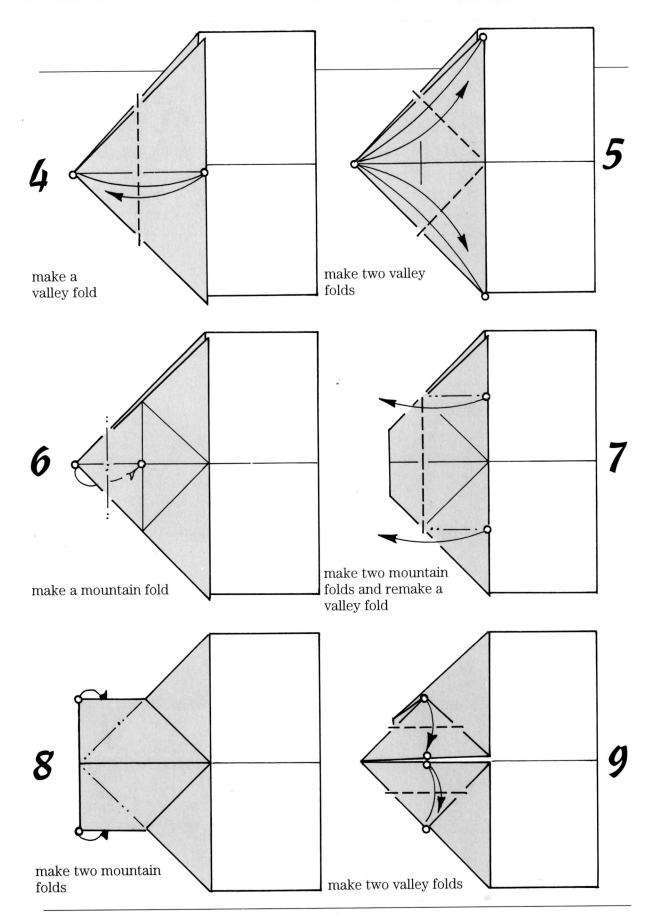

4

make a
valley fold

5

make two valley
folds

6

make a mountain fold

7

make two mountain
folds and remake a
valley fold

8

make two mountain
folds

9

make two valley folds

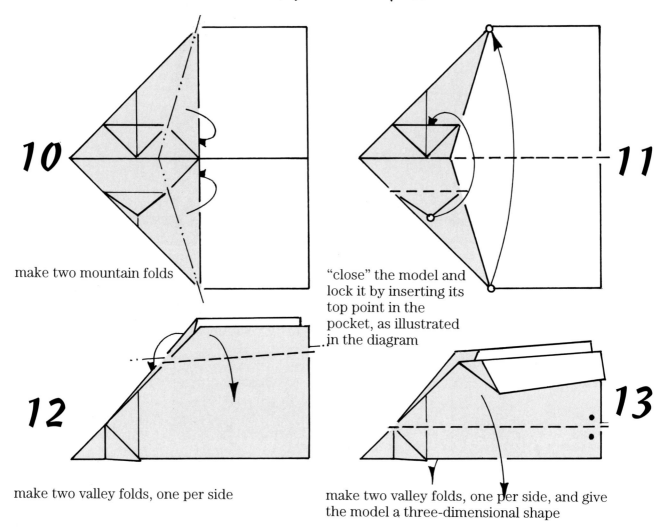

10 make two mountain folds

11 "close" the model and lock it by inserting its top point in the pocket, as illustrated in the diagram

12 make two valley folds, one per side

13 make two valley folds, one per side, and give the model a three-dimensional shape

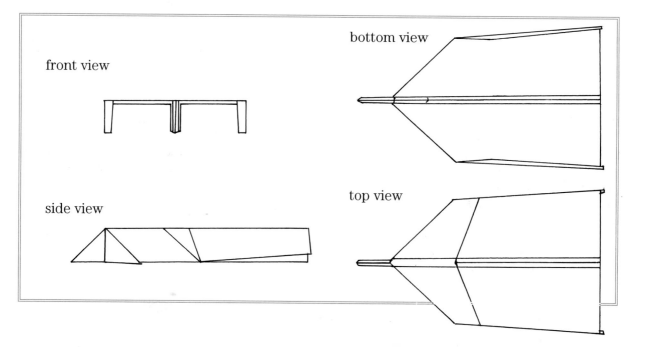

front view

side view

bottom view

top view

Space taxi

A model for the distance category

Type of paper:........	extra strong
Level:..............	intermediate to advanced
Launch:............	medium
Flight path:.........	straight line, fast
Behavior:...........	tendency to veer
Stability:	good

*T*his is similar to the previous models. The smaller wing surface, the vertical fin, and the absence of vertical surfaces at the end of the wings make this model sensitive to problems with construction. In fact, the thickness of several layers of paper may make it difficult for you to create a perfect model. Pay particular attention to the vertical fin. Check to be sure it is symmetrical. If it is not, the model will turn almost continuously in flight.

You'll launch this model the same way you launched the previous ones: straight and horizontal. If you launch it upwards, the model will quickly stall and have difficulty adjusting its flight path.

Although this is a little complicated to make, all you'll really need is a little patience and attention.

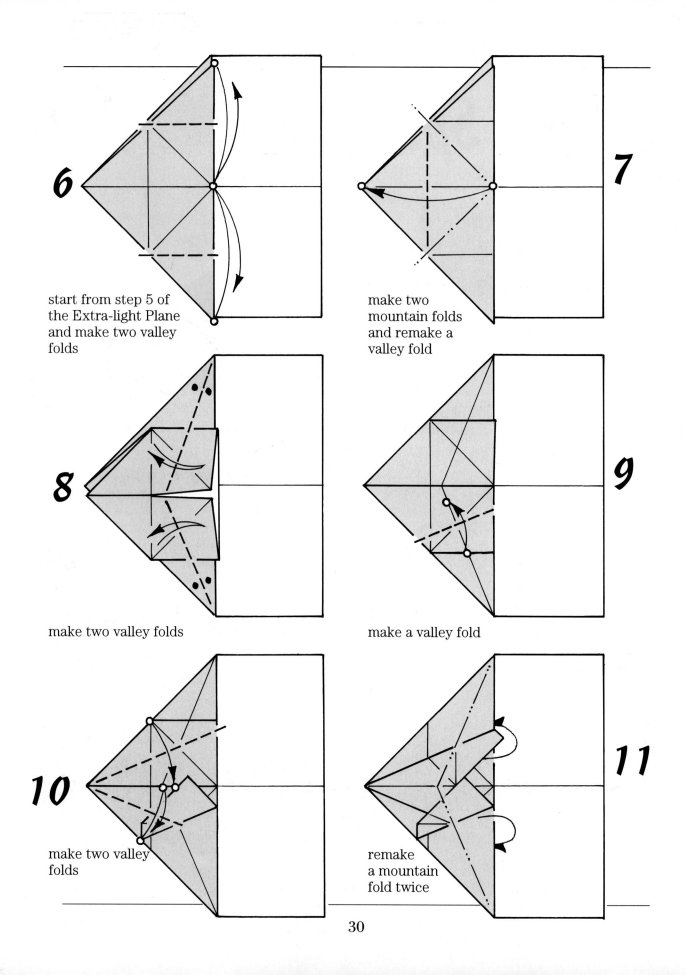

6 start from step 5 of
the Extra-light Plane
and make two valley
folds

7 make two
mountain folds
and remake a
valley fold

8 make two valley folds

9 make a valley fold

10 make two valley
folds

11 remake
a mountain
fold twice

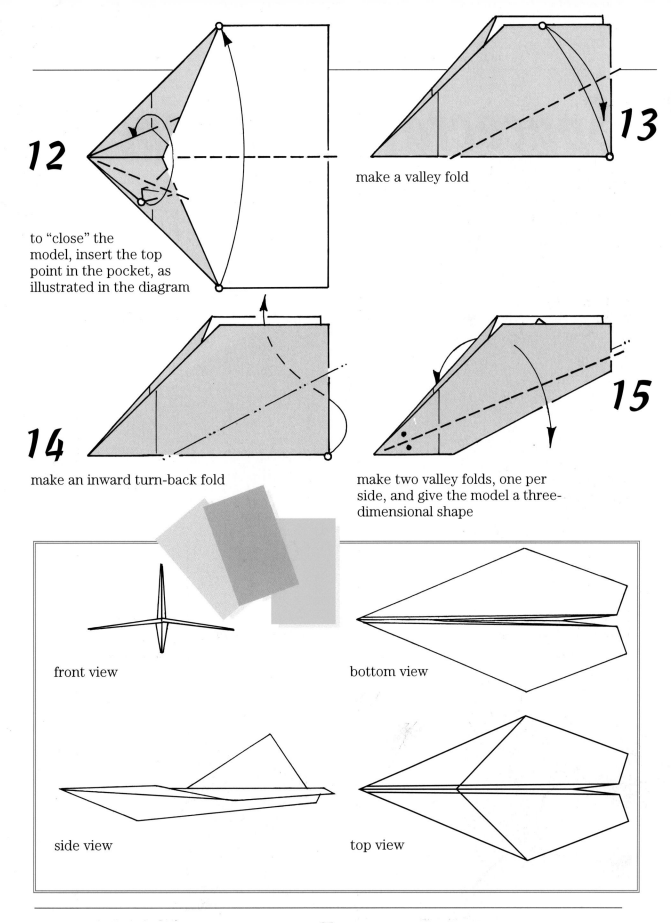

12

to "close" the model, insert the top point in the pocket, as illustrated in the diagram

13

make a valley fold

14

make an inward turn-back fold

15

make two valley folds, one per side, and give the model a three-dimensional shape

front view

bottom view

side view

top view

31

Spacecraft "Cassiopeia"

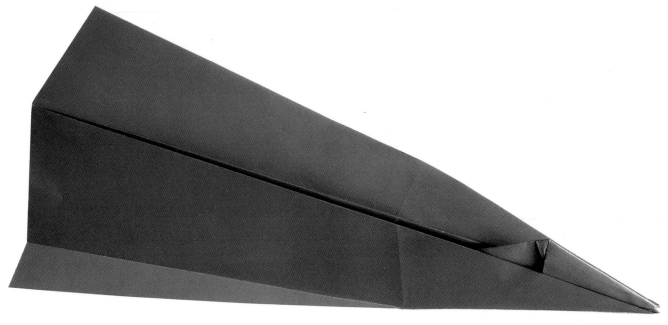

A model for the distance category

Type of paper: .... extra strong

Level: .... easy

Launch: .... slow, accompanied

Flight path: .... straight line, slow

Behavior: .... slight tendency
to nose-dive

Stability: .... good

*T*his model is easy to make and launch, and you are assured good results. Step 8 is a little tricky because the long fold may turn out crooked and not symmetrical on the two wings. You might want to use a ruler for this step.

Launch this model rather slowly and tilt it slightly upwards. In some cases, this model tends to nose-dive, but you can compensate for this by slightly folding the trailing edge upwards, creating two flaps.

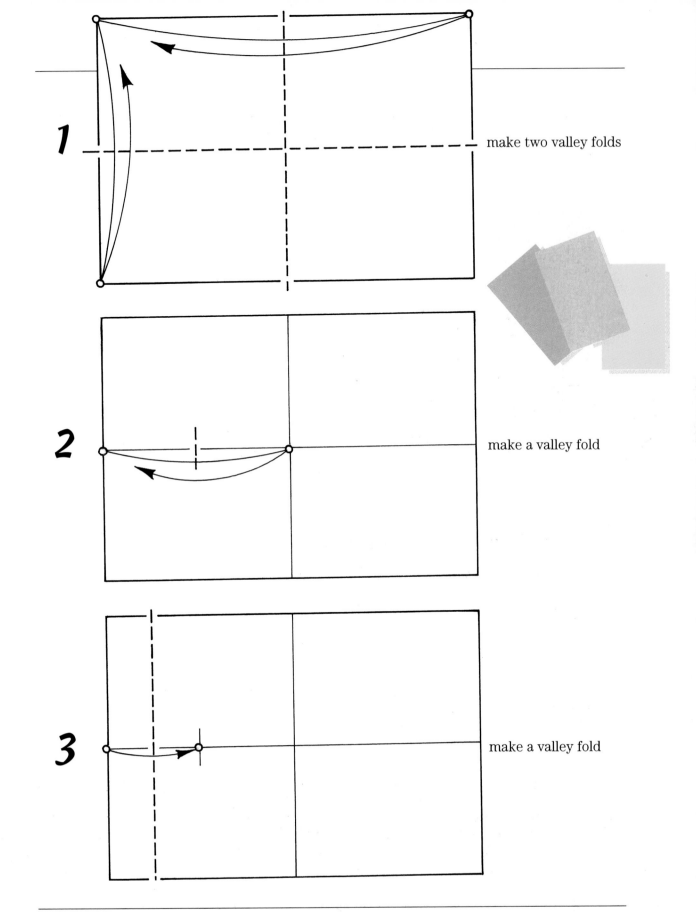

1   make two valley folds

2   make a valley fold

3   make a valley fold

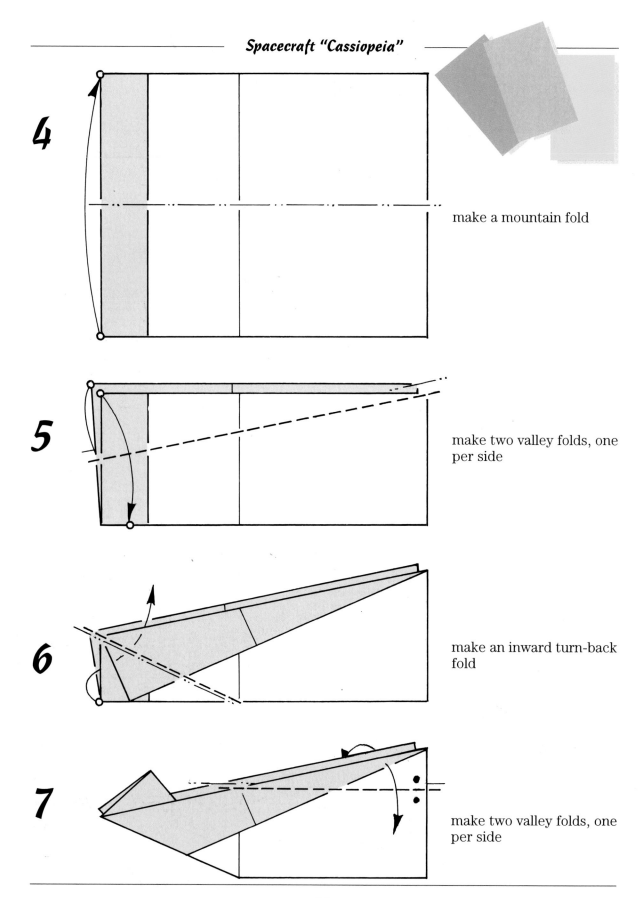

4 make a mountain fold

5 make two valley folds, one per side

6 make an inward turn-back fold

7 make two valley folds, one per side

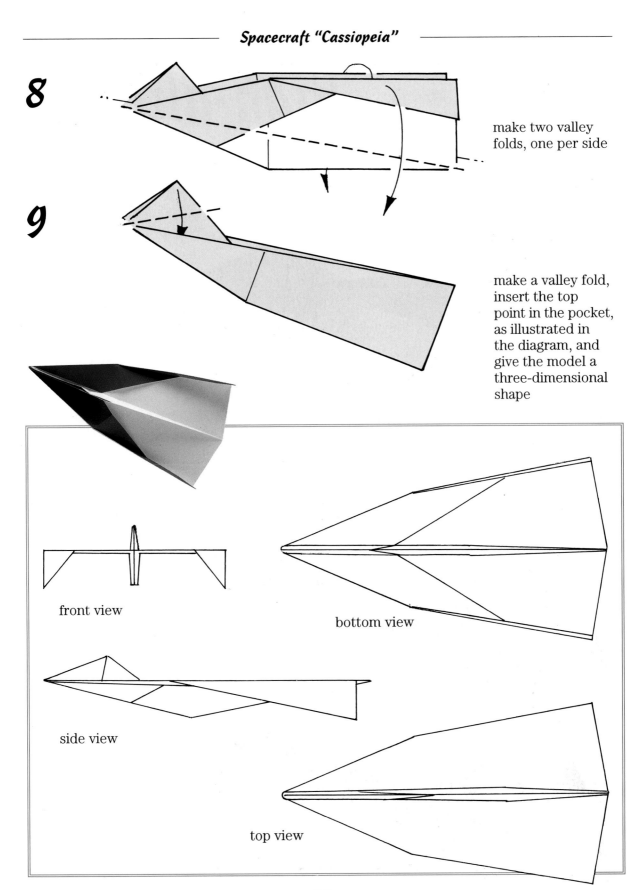

8

make two valley folds, one per side

9

make a valley fold, insert the top point in the pocket, as illustrated in the diagram, and give the model a three-dimensional shape

front view

bottom view

side view

top view

High-altitude reconnaissance plane

A model for the distance category

Type of paper:	extra strong
Level:	intermediate
Launch:	slow to medium
Flight path:	straight line, slow
Behavior:	tendency to roll
Stability:	good

This model has elegant lines and uses interesting folding techniques. Although these folds are not difficult, small mistakes in proportions can cause unsatisfactory flight behavior. Often, for example, this model has problems with its first flight, wheeling on its own longitudinal or vertical axis. However, you can correct this.

First, check the symmetry of the rudder unit; then, give the wing a slight angle. Should the craft remain unstable, turning and pitching violently, then you'll need to increase the tab area of the wing extremities with another fold.

You can correct any tendency to pitch by opening small flaps on the trailing edge of the wings.

At this point, the model's flight depends on the force used in launching it. That force can't be too weak or the model will fall, but it can't be too strong or the model will pitch and go into a stall.

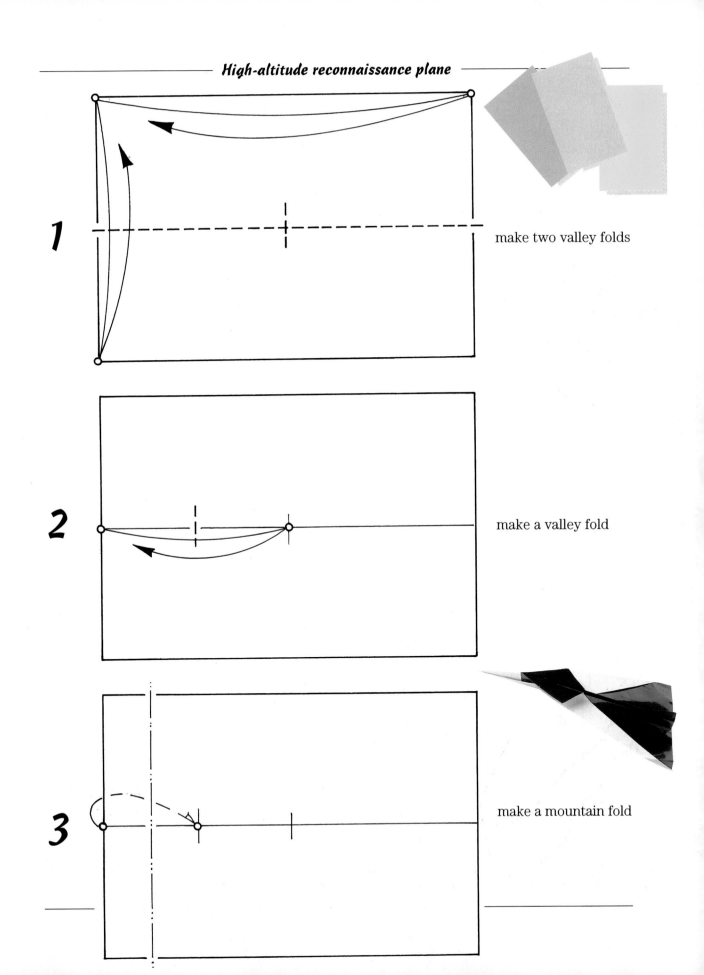

1 make two valley folds

2 make a valley fold

3 make a mountain fold

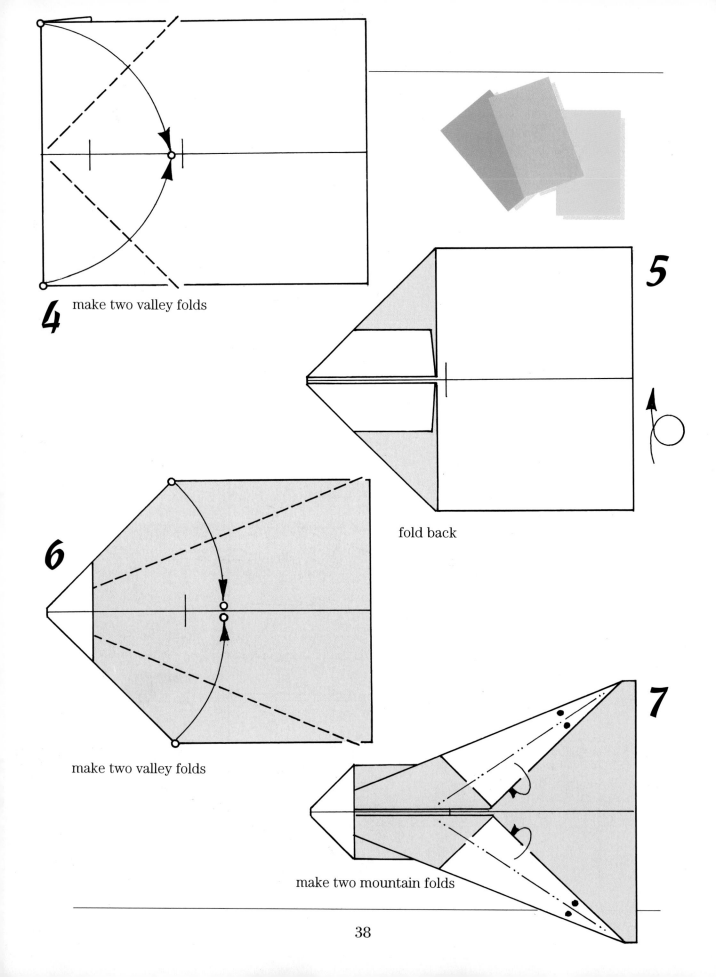

4 make two valley folds

5 fold back

6 make two valley folds

7 make two mountain folds

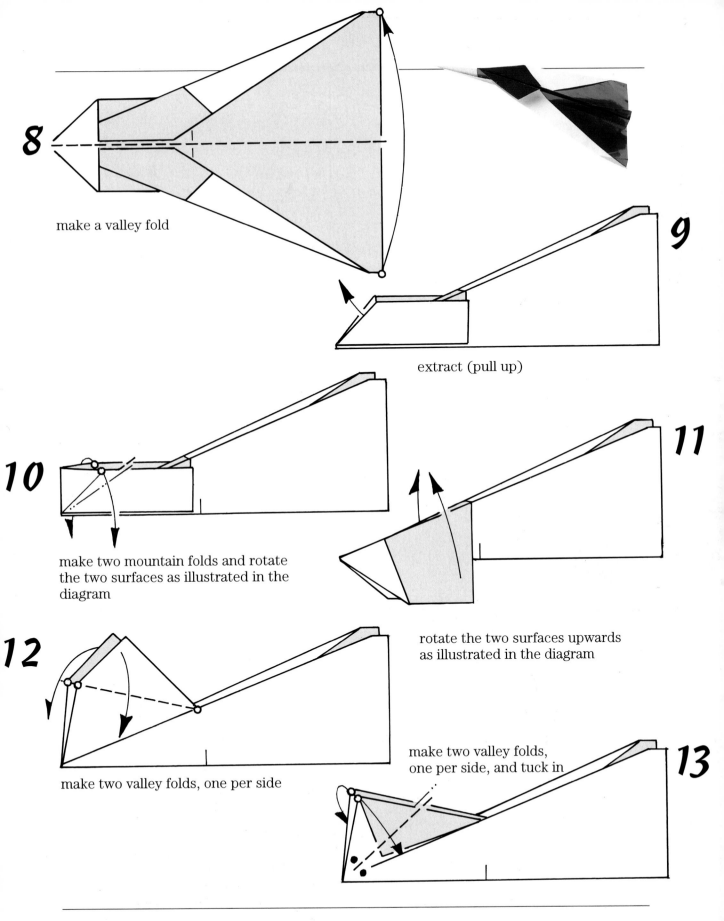

8 make a valley fold

9 extract (pull up)

10 make two mountain folds and rotate the two surfaces as illustrated in the diagram

11 rotate the two surfaces upwards as illustrated in the diagram

12 make two valley folds, one per side

13 make two valley folds, one per side, and tuck in

39

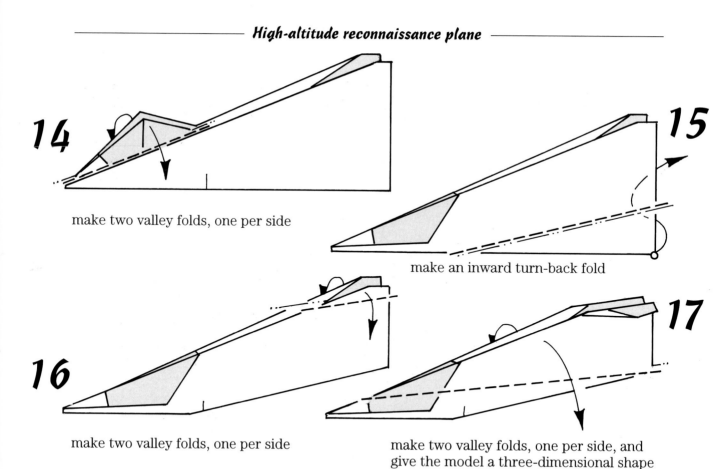

14 make two valley folds, one per side

15 make an inward turn-back fold

16 make two valley folds, one per side

17 make two valley folds, one per side, and give the model a three-dimensional shape

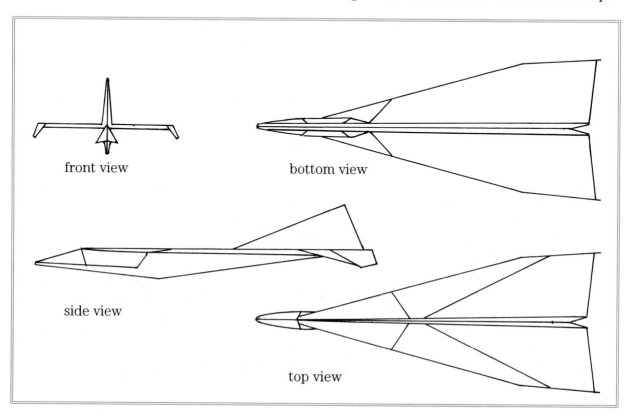

front view

bottom view

side view

top view

Stealth reconnaissance plane

A model for the distance category

Type of paper:	extra strong
Level:	intermediate
Launch:	strong
Flight path:	straight line, fast
Behavior:	tendency to veer
Stability:	good (after corrections)

This model has a big name, but it deserves it. The design, which includes a number of slanting folds on multifolded layers of paper, can produce some inaccuracies. The wing, for example, could turn out to have a smaller fold than indicated. But don't panic; all is not lost. Although you'll want to keep a constant eye on the symmetry, you may change the proportions, within certain limits.

The launch requires attention. This model, unlike most of the previous ones, isn't locked, so it tends to open up, particularly when it hits an obstacle. Therefore, you should restore it to its original shape before each launch.

You can correct the tendency to turn by controlling the small triangular edges at the end of the winglets. You'll need a somewhat strong launch, but, as with all models needing some force, after the initial thrust, it is inclined to pitch. You can remedy this tendency with two flaps on the wing's trailing edge and a careful launch.

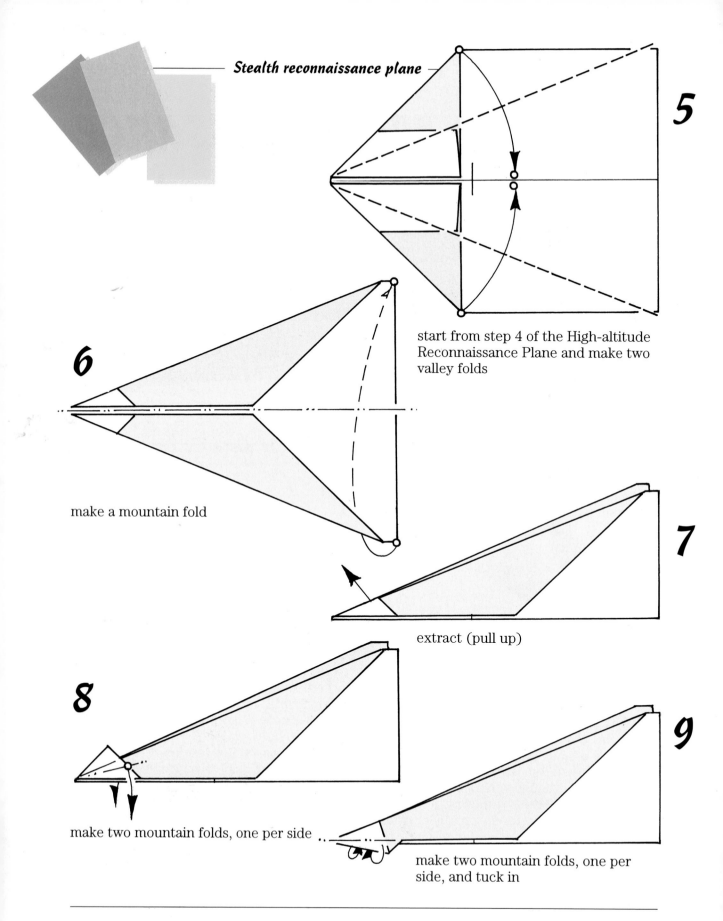

Stealth reconnaissance plane

5

start from step 4 of the High-altitude Reconnaissance Plane and make two valley folds

6

make a mountain fold

7

extract (pull up)

8

make two mountain folds, one per side

9

make two mountain folds, one per side, and tuck in

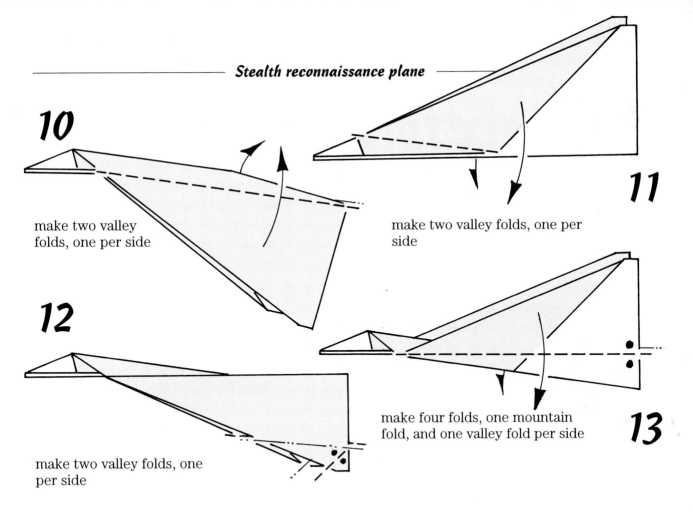

10 make two valley folds, one per side

11 make two valley folds, one per side

12 make two valley folds, one per side

13 make four folds, one mountain fold, and one valley fold per side

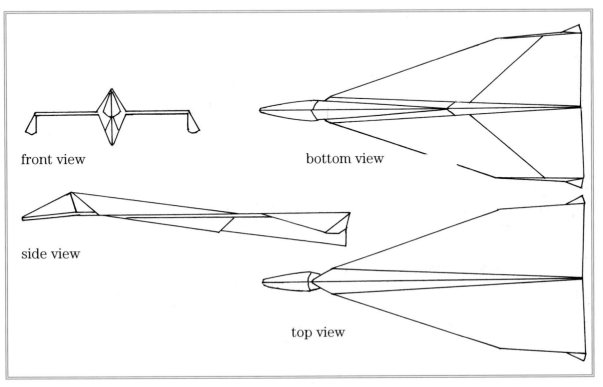

front view

bottom view

side view

top view

Spaceship "Raccoon"

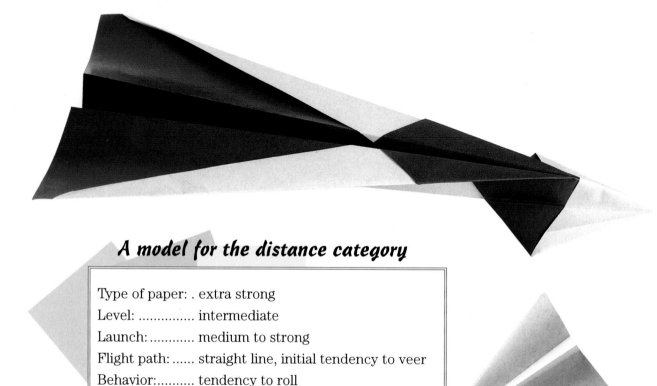

A model for the distance category

> Type of paper: . extra strong
> Level: .... intermediate
> Launch: .... medium to strong
> Flight path: ...... straight line, initial tendency to veer
> Behavior:.......... tendency to roll
> Stability:........... good

*T*he unusual shape of this fine model with its two front whiskers puts it in a special category.

In this case, though each step is not that difficult, the complexity of the folding may lead to mistakes. However, if you maintain the symmetry, the flight will turn out well.

The model tends to unfold in flight, but even this does not present significant problems. The flight characteristics depend essentially on the main front wing angles. In particular, the more the two front wings incline downwards, the more stable the model is. By changing the angle of the wings and unfolding small flaps on the trailing edge of the main wing, you can change the flight behavior. This model requires a medium to strong launch, but after the initial thrust, it tends to crash.

Using suitable flaps can produce a steady flight, but the trick lies in measuring the correct amount of launch force.

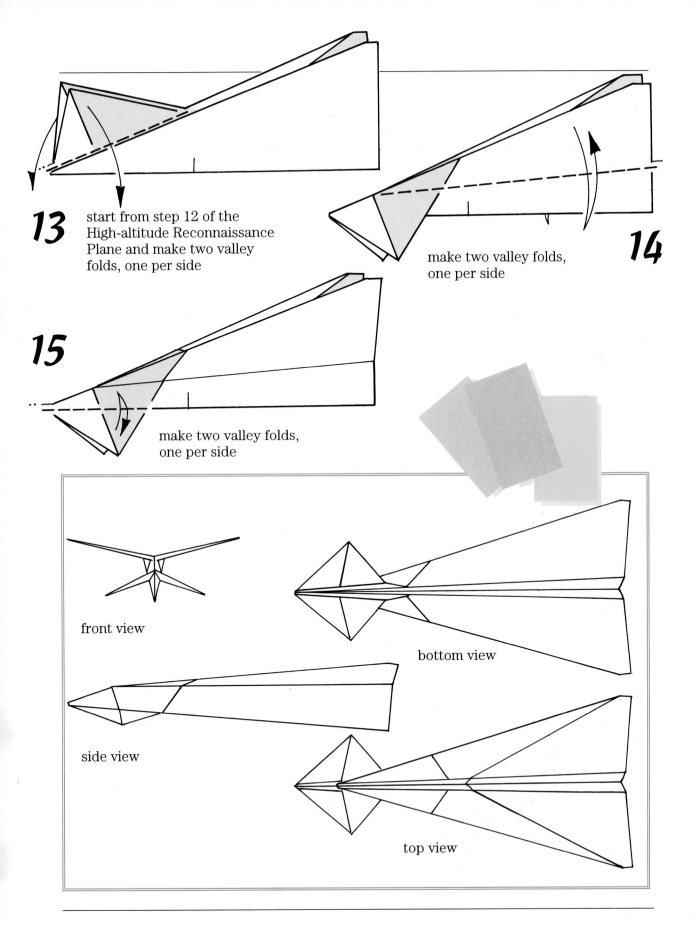

13 start from step 12 of the High-altitude Reconnaissance Plane and make two valley folds, one per side

14 make two valley folds, one per side

15 make two valley folds, one per side

front view

bottom view

side view

top view

Seaplane

A model for the distance category

Type of paper:	extra strong
Level:	intermediate
Launch:	medium to strong
Flight path:	straight line
Behavior:	level flight
Stability:	medium

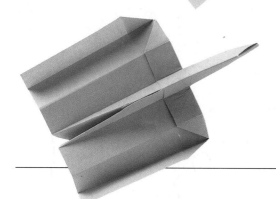

*T*his model has a tendency to pitch and turn. You can correct the pitching by folding two flaps on the wing's trailing edge which will produce a nose-up effect.
The tendency to turn is usually the result of not aligning the winglets properly.

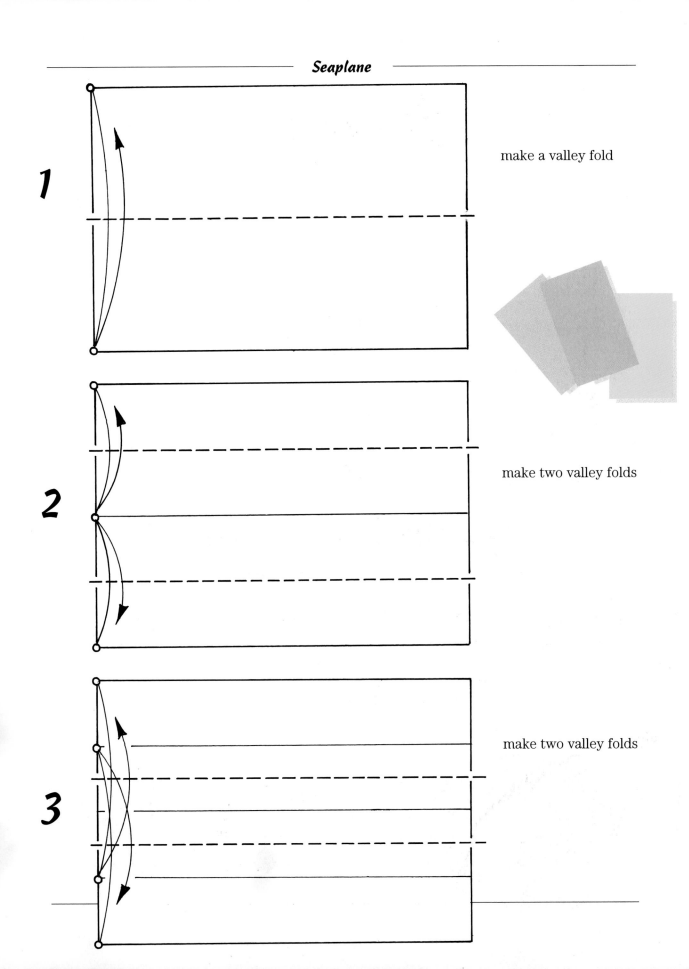

1 make a valley fold

2 make two valley folds

3 make two valley folds

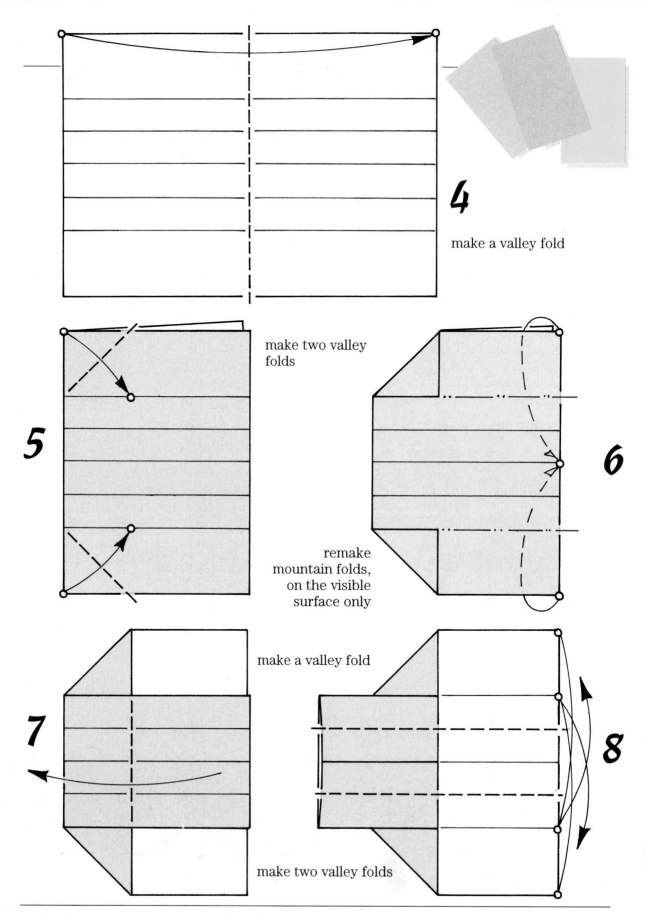

4

make a valley fold

5

make two valley folds

6

remake mountain folds, on the visible surface only

7

make a valley fold

make two valley folds

8

9

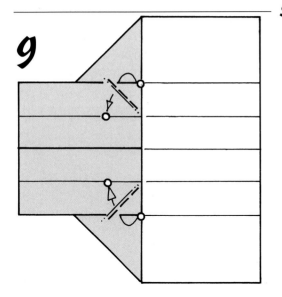

make two inward turn-back folds

10

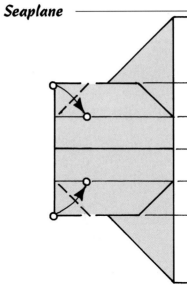

make two valley folds

11

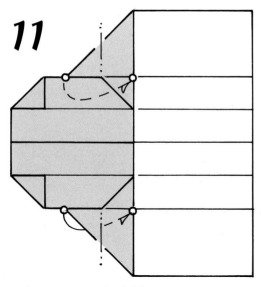

make a mountain fold

12

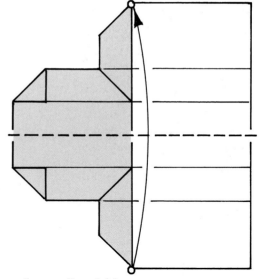

make a valley fold

13

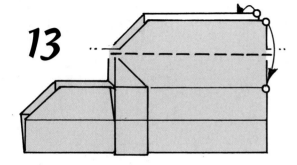

make two valley folds, one per side

14

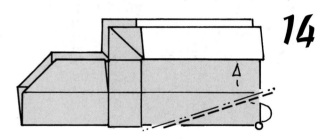

make an inward turn-back fold

15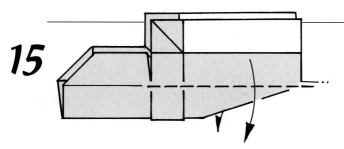

make two valley folds, one per side

16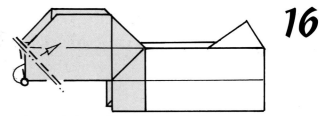

make an internal inside-out fold

17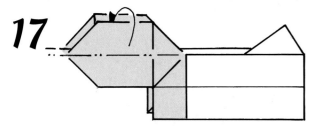

remake a mountain fold and tuck in
to lock the model

18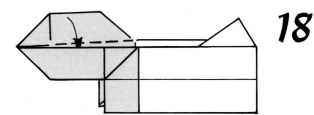

remake the valley fold, tuck in, and give the
model a three-dimensional shape

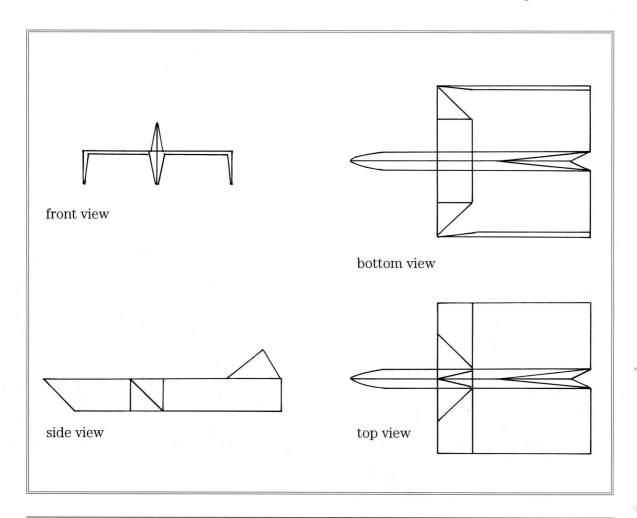

front view

bottom view

side view

top view

Trainer craft

A model for the distance category

Type of paper:	extra strong
Level:	intermediate
Launch:	strong to very strong
Flight path:	straight line; initially nose up
Behavior:	level flight
Stability:	medium to good

As is the case with the previous model, this craft tends to pitch, but it doesn't turn. You can correct the pitching with two flaps to produce a suitable nose-up effect. Using a tail as ballast will also work.

When the launch is strong, the model noses slightly upwards, resulting in a flutter (the craft seems to beat its wings). The flutter, which is dangerous to real airplanes, isn't a problem with this model. The same is true of the previous model.

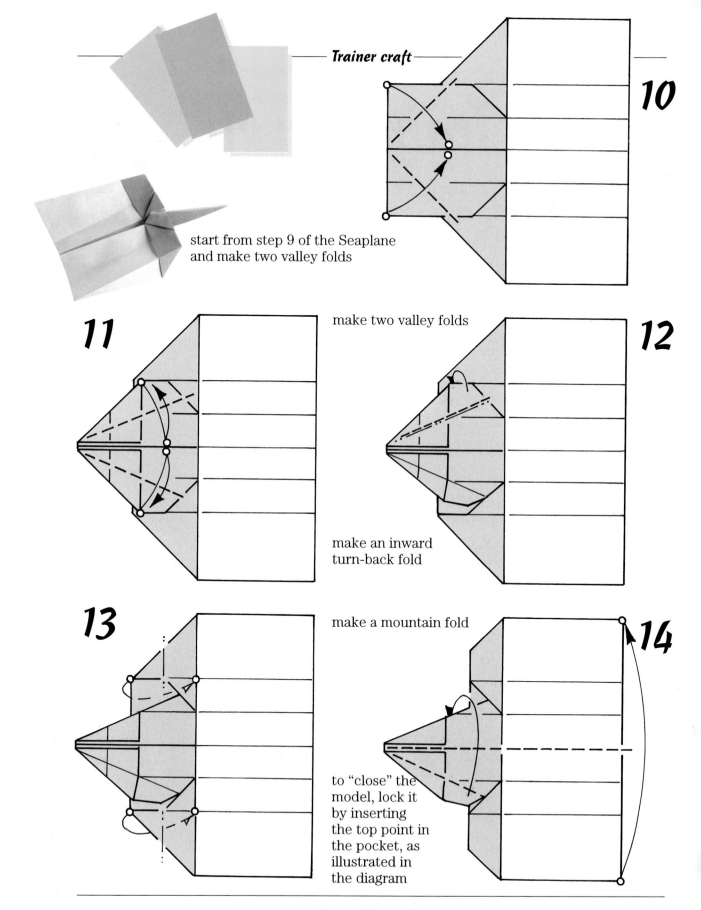

10

start from step 9 of the Seaplane
and make two valley folds

11

make two valley folds

12

make an inward
turn-back fold

13

make a mountain fold

14

to "close" the
model, lock it
by inserting
the top point in
the pocket, as
illustrated in
the diagram

15

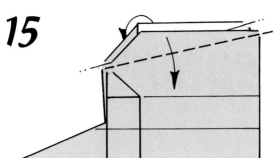

make two valley folds, one per side

16

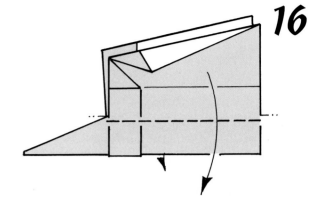

make two valley folds, one per side, and give the model a three-dimensional shape

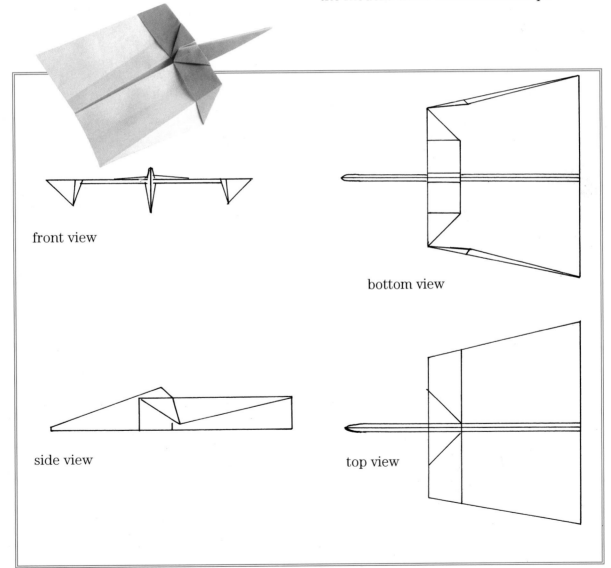

front view

side view

bottom view

top view

Interceptor

A model for the distance and acrobatics category

Type of paper:	extra strong
Level:	intermediate to advanced
Launch:	medium
Flight path:	straight line
Behavior:	level flight
Stability:	medium

This model tends to pitch and to fly upside down. The possible solutions are to unfold two flaps on the wing's trailing edge and to add ballast to the center of gravity. Unless, of course, you're willing to accept the model's strange, elegant upside-down flight.

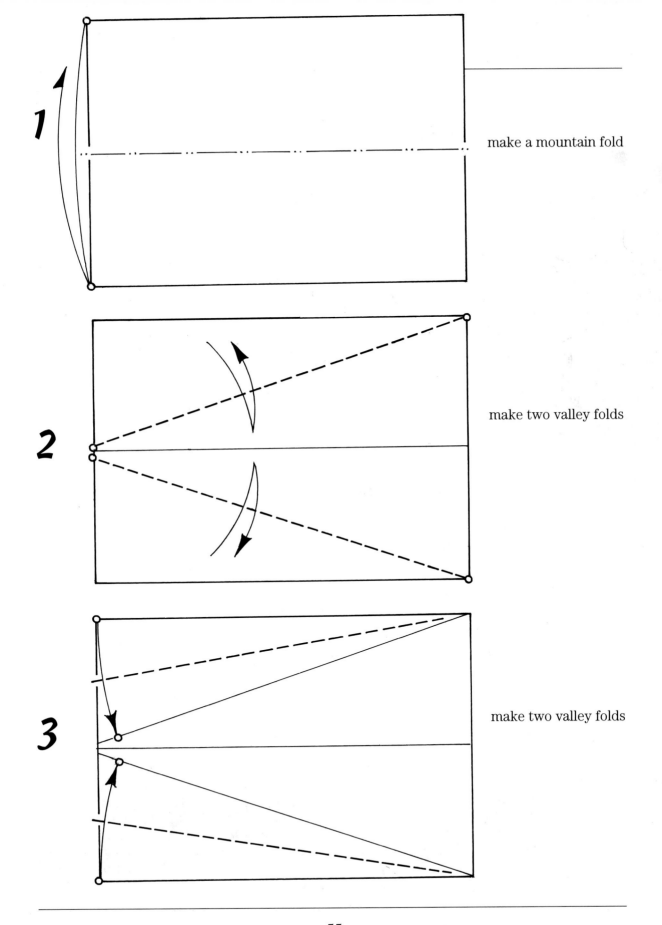

1   make a mountain fold

2   make two valley folds

3   make two valley folds

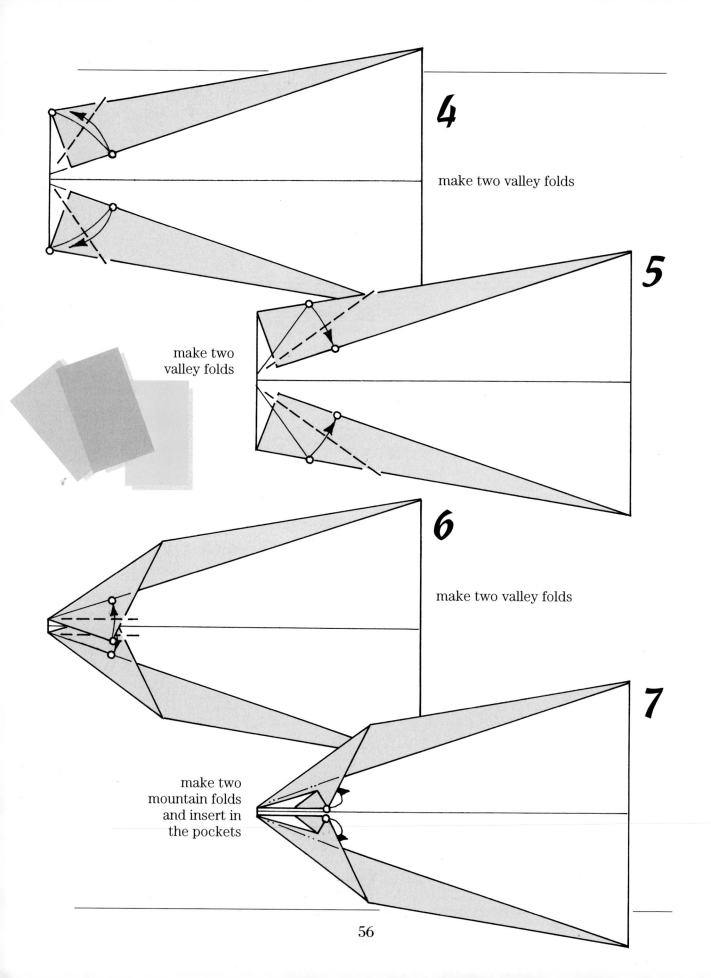

4

make two valley folds

5

make two
valley folds

6

make two valley folds

7

make two
mountain folds
and insert in
the pockets

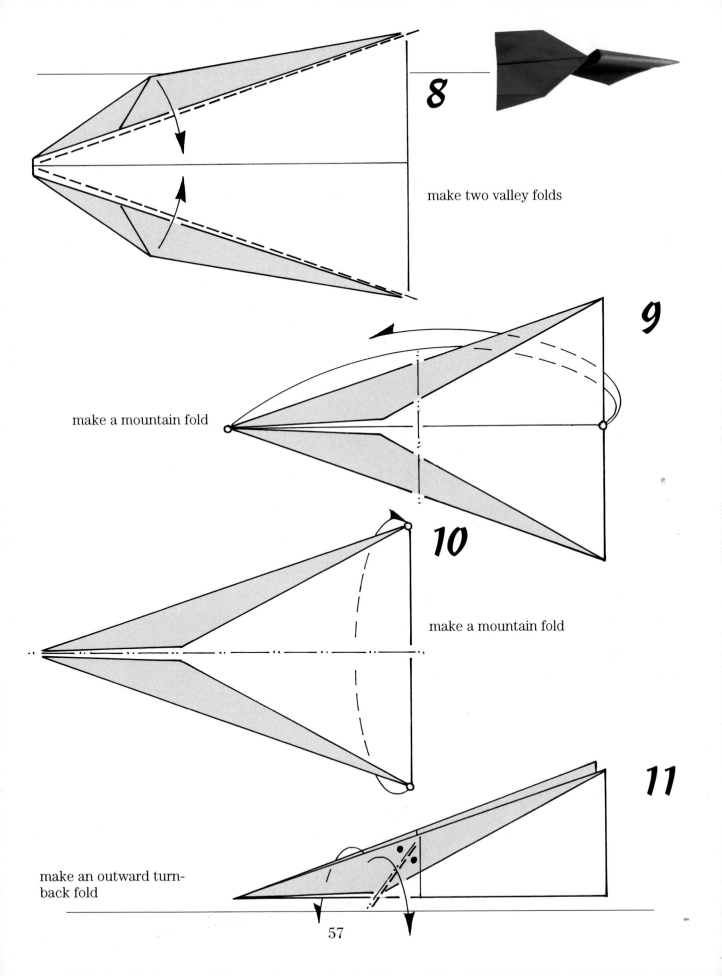

8

make two valley folds

9

make a mountain fold

10

make a mountain fold

11

make an outward turn-
back fold

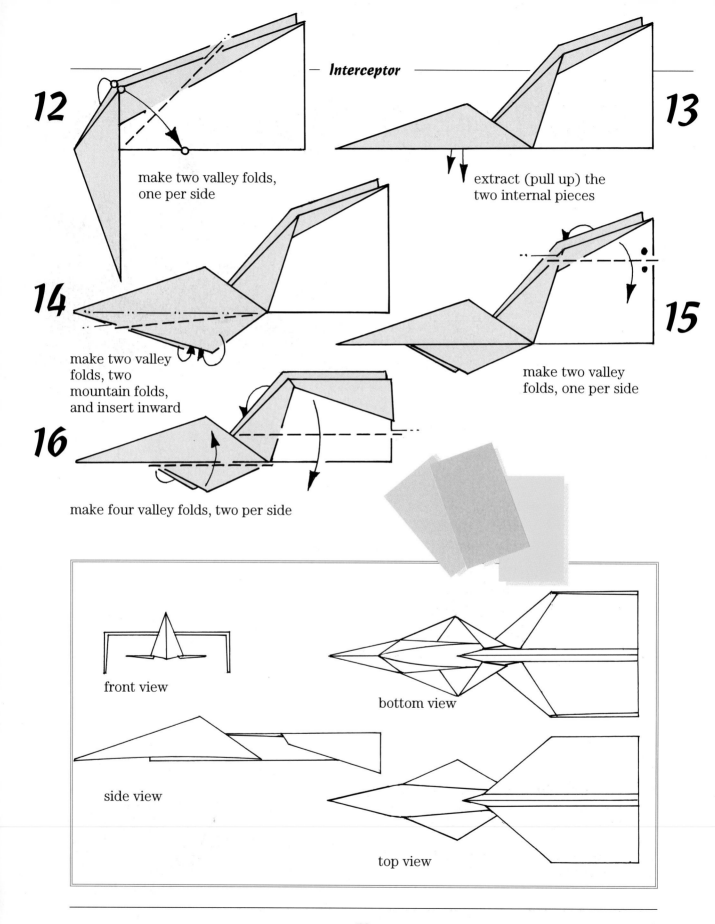

12 make two valley folds, one per side

13 extract (pull up) the two internal pieces

14 make two valley folds, two mountain folds, and insert inward

15 make two valley folds, one per side

16 make four valley folds, two per side

front view

bottom view

side view

top view

Spacecraft "Berenice"

A model for the duration category

Type of paper:	extra strong
Level:	intermediate to advanced
Launch:	slow to medium
Flight path:	straight line
Behavior:	nose-up attitude
Stability:	good

*T*hanks to its different weight distribution and greater wing area, this model flies better than the previous one and doesn't fly upside down.
In this case, too, you should unfold a pair of flaps to give added control.

14

start from step 13 of the Interceptor and make two valley folds, one per side

15

make two valley folds, one per side

16

make two valley folds, one per side

17

make two valley folds, one per side, and give the model a three-dimensional shape

front view

bottom view

side view

top view

Alien spaceship UZ RK

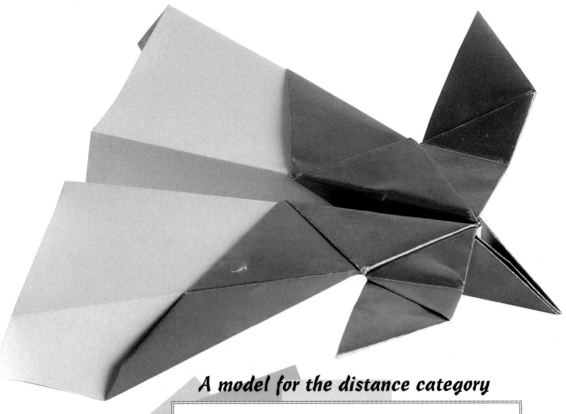

A model for the distance category

Type of paper:	extra strong
Level:	easy to intermediate
Launch:............................	medium
Flight path:	straight line with
	initial tendency to veer
Behavior:..........................	nose-up attitude
Stability:...........................	good

*T*he only problem with this model is that you might place the wings at different angles than the picture indicates. You can offset the slight tendency to pitch by unfolding a pair of flaps on the trailing edge of the main wing.

This will create a paper that is balanced and stable.

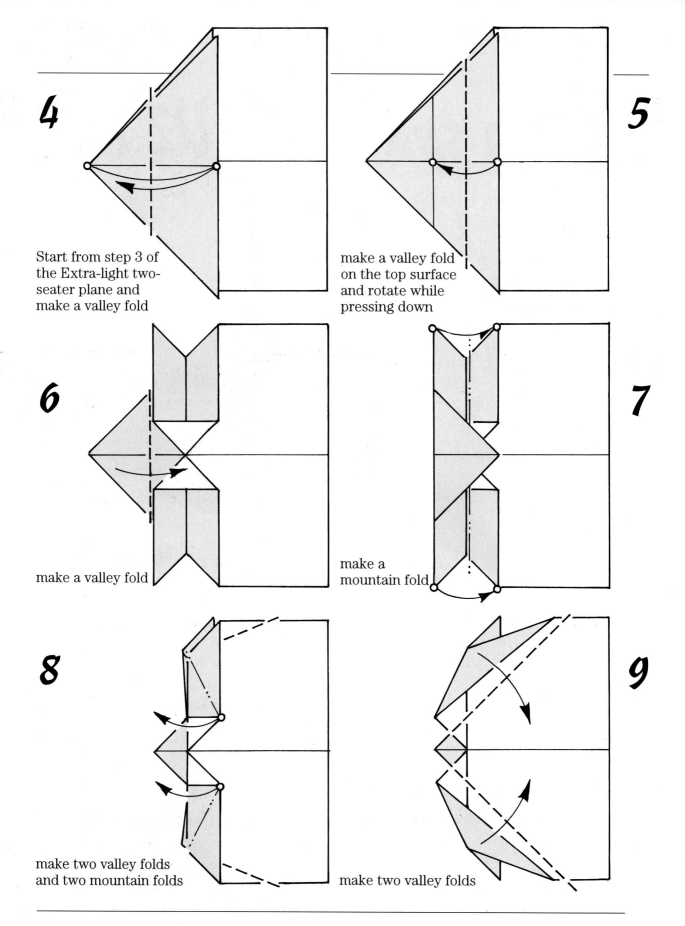

4

Start from step 3 of
the Extra-light two-
seater plane and
make a valley fold

5

make a valley fold
on the top surface
and rotate while
pressing down

6

make a valley fold

7

make a
mountain fold

8

make two valley folds
and two mountain folds

9

make two valley folds

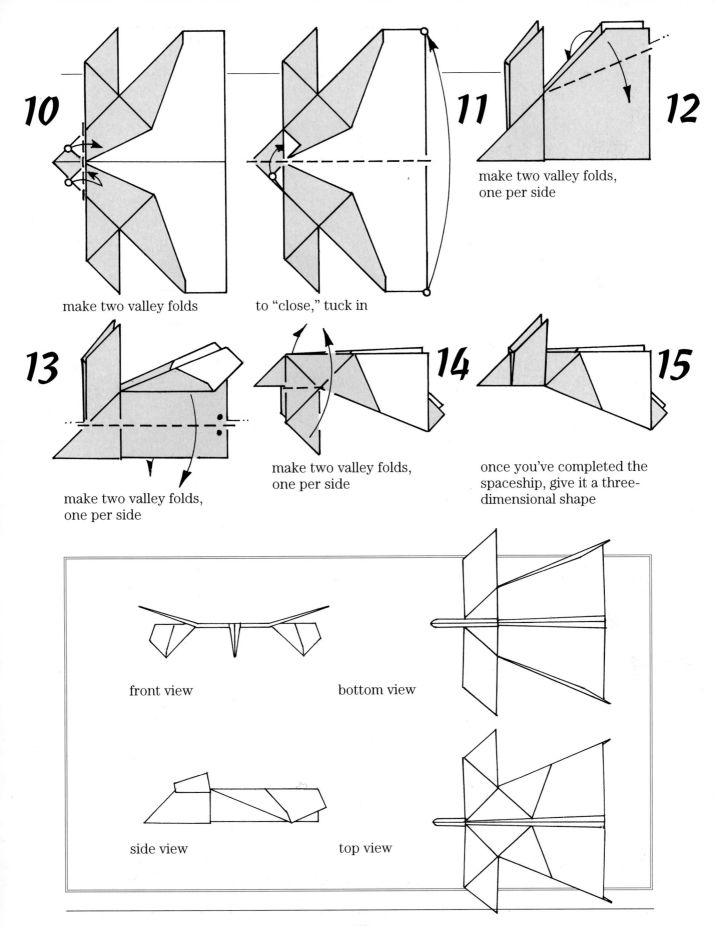

10

make two valley folds

11

to "close," tuck in

12

make two valley folds,
one per side

13

make two valley folds,
one per side

14

make two valley folds,
one per side

15

once you've completed the
spaceship, give it a three-
dimensional shape

front view

bottom view

side view

top view

Alien spacecraft

This is a truly excellent model that flies very efficiently.

If it has a tendency to nose-dive in the final phase of the flight, reduce the extension of the winglets by unfolding two small flaps on the trailing edge of the wing or by increasing the wing surface.

A model for the distance category

Type of paper:	extra strong
Level:	easy
Launch:	slow to medium
Flight path:	straight line
Behavior:	level flight
Stability:	good

1

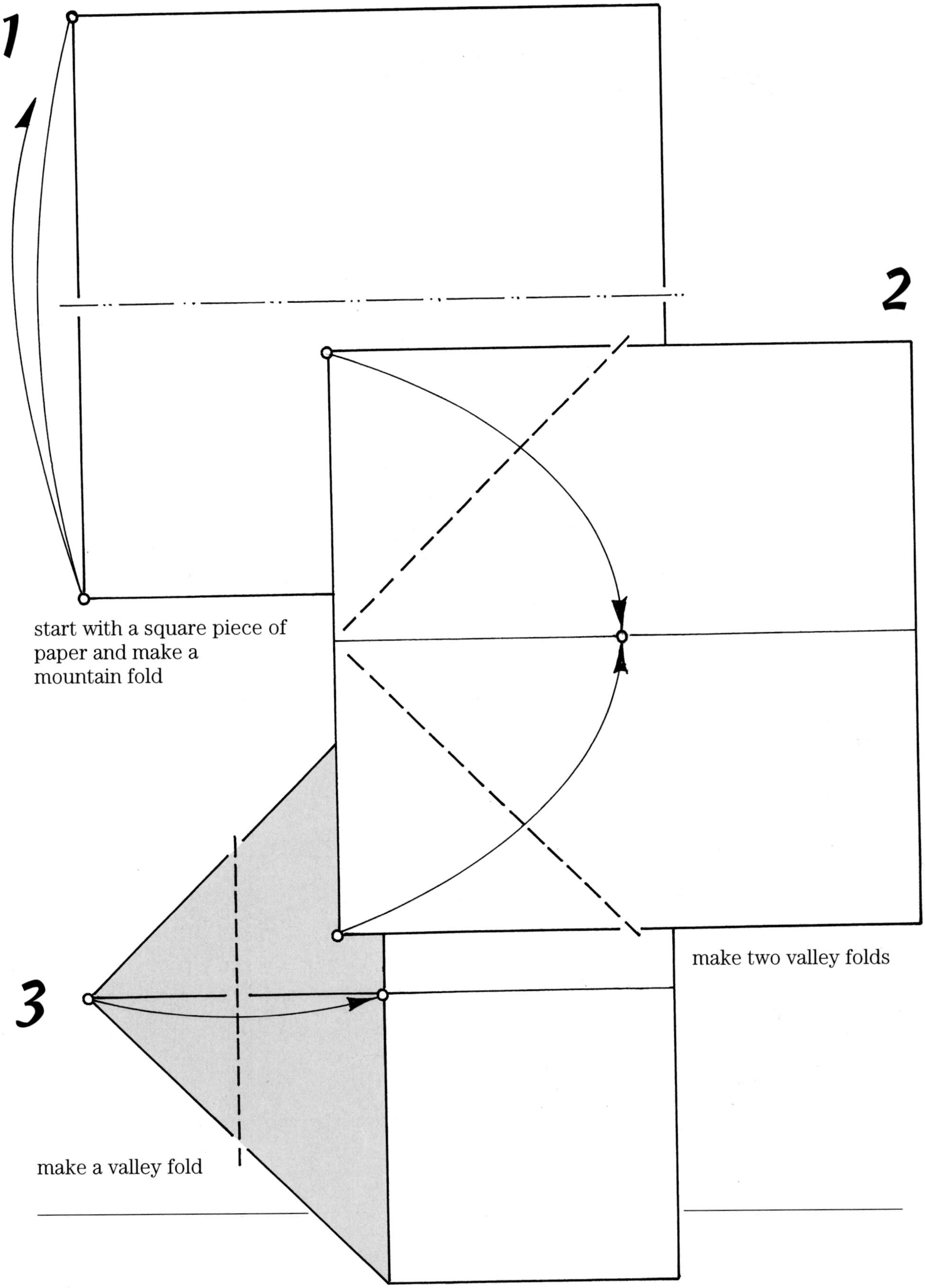

start with a square piece of
paper and make a
mountain fold

2

make two valley folds

3

make a valley fold

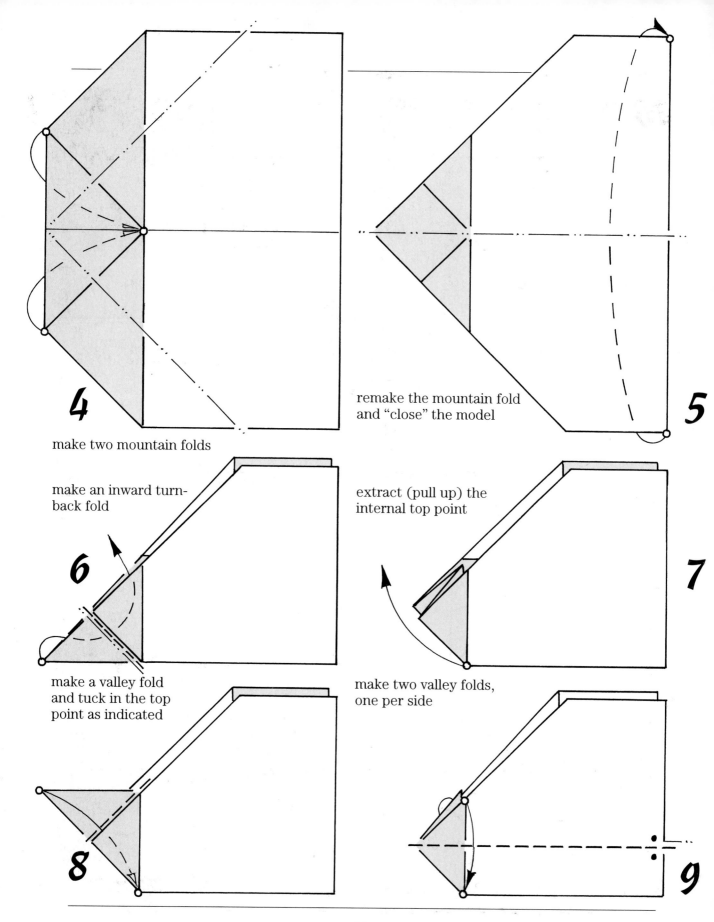

4

make two mountain folds

5

remake the mountain fold
and "close" the model

6

make an inward turn-
back fold

7

extract (pull up) the
internal top point

8

make a valley fold
and tuck in the top
point as indicated

9

make two valley folds,
one per side

10

11

once you've completed the model, give it a three-dimensional shape

make two valley folds, one per side

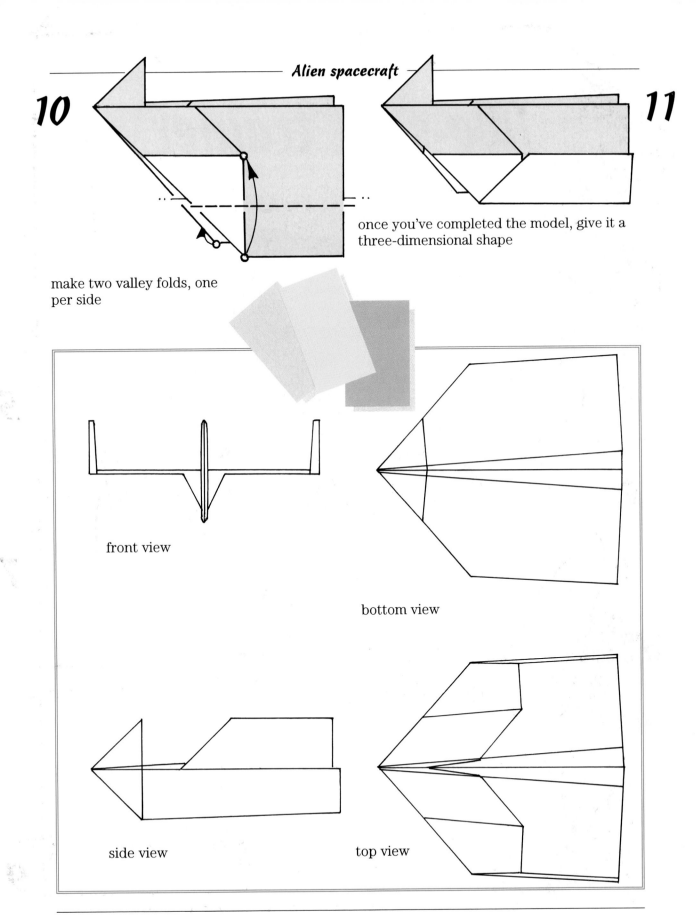

front view

bottom view

side view

top view

Two-seat trainer

A model for the distance category

Type of paper:	extra strong
Level:	easy to intermediate
Launch:	slow to medium
Flight path:	straight line
Behavior:	level flight
Stability:	good

*T*his model has good flying characteristics; however, it is very sensitive to launching problems.

In other words, you won't need to correct the aerodynamics of the plane, but you must launch the plane carefully, paying special attention to launching it in right direction.

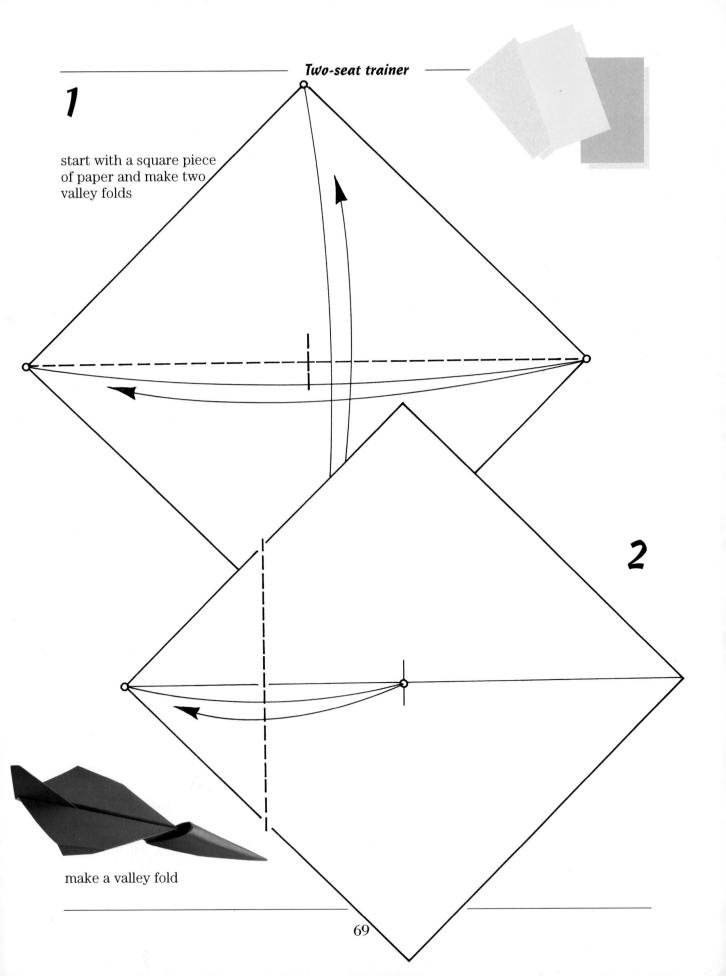

1

start with a square piece
of paper and make two
valley folds

2

make a valley fold

69

3

make a valley fold

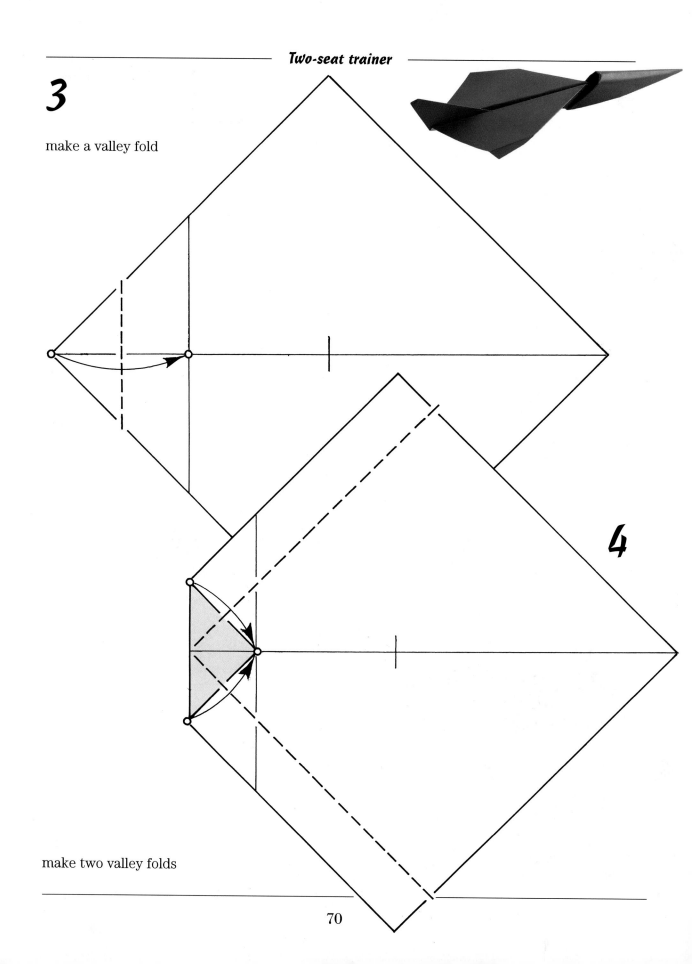

4

make two valley folds

5

make two valley folds

6

make a mountain fold

7

remake the
mountain fold and
"close" the model

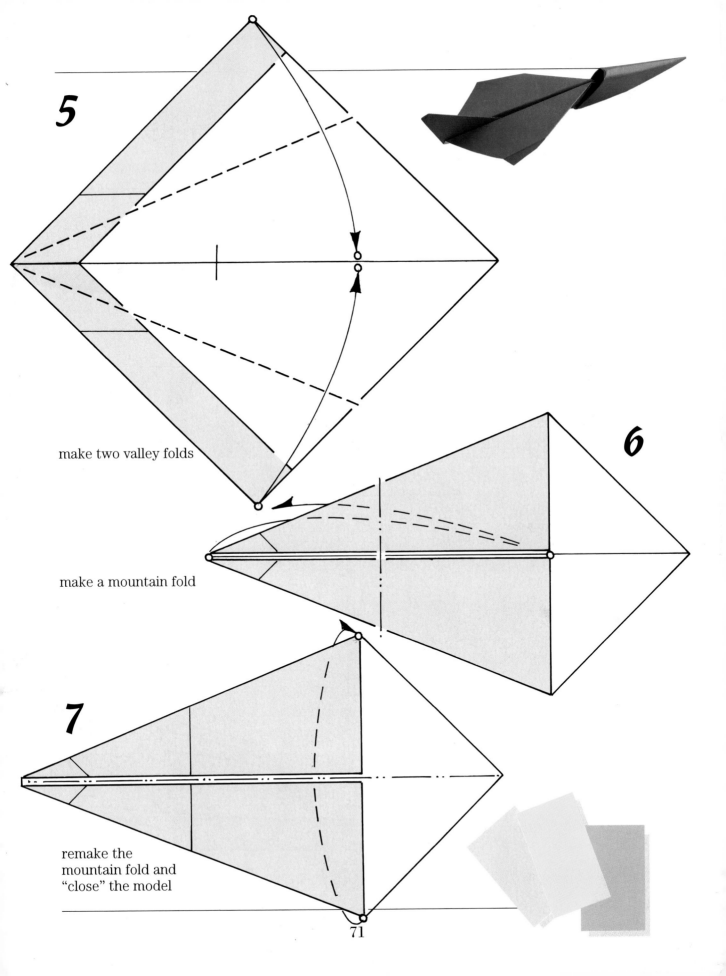

71

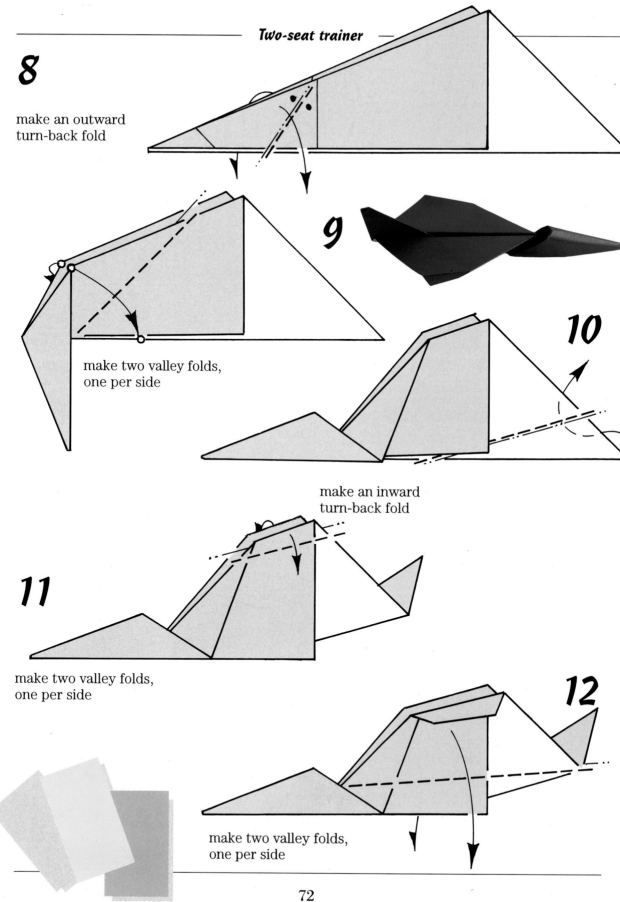

Two-seat trainer

8

make an outward
turn-back fold

9

make two valley folds,
one per side

10

make an inward
turn-back fold

11

make two valley folds,
one per side

12

make two valley folds,
one per side

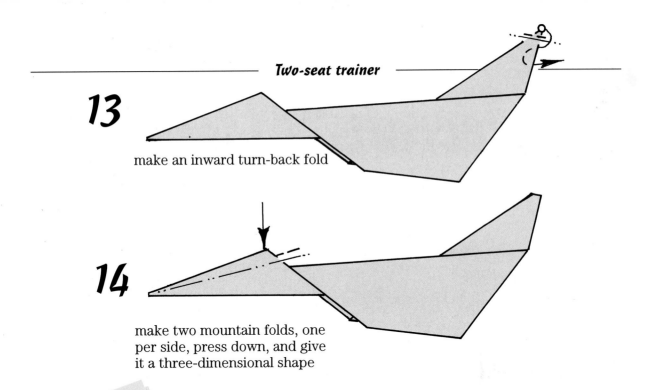

13 make an inward turn-back fold

14 make two mountain folds, one per side, press down, and give it a three-dimensional shape

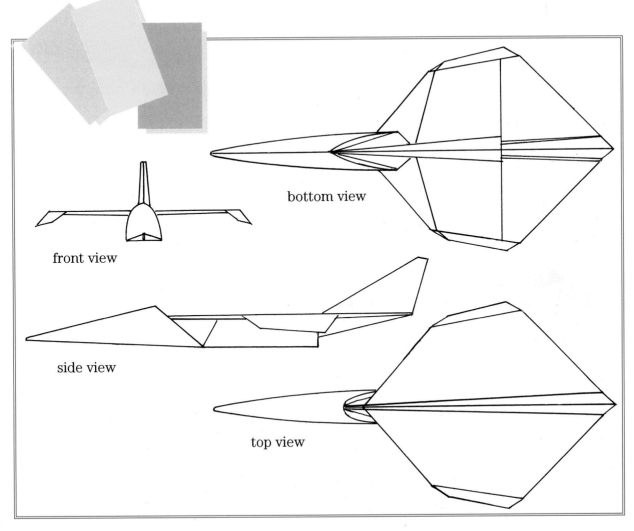

front view

bottom view

side view

top view

Spacecraft "Aldebran"

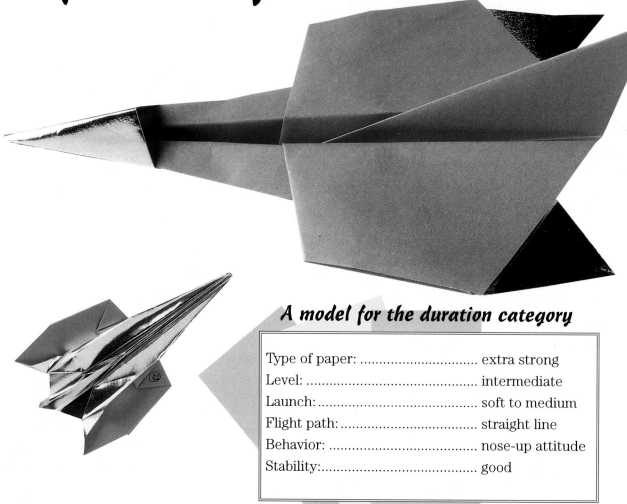

A model for the duration category

Type of paper:	extra strong
Level:	intermediate
Launch:	soft to medium
Flight path:	straight line
Behavior:	nose-up attitude
Stability:	good

*T*his is one of those models that is almost perfectly balanced. In fact, without modifying it in any way, you can produce excellent results simply by flicking your wrist while launching. And you'll only need a few trial attempts to discover the correct movement.

While in flight, the model is somewhat nose up. It resembles the Concorde during the takeoff and landing stages. It never goes into a stall because the wings present some sloping areas that act as an aerodynamic break, reducing every hint of instability. Thus, there is no reason to try to close the folds with tape or glue. On the contrary, instability problems may sometimes arise when you close the rudder unit or the bow hood with tape.

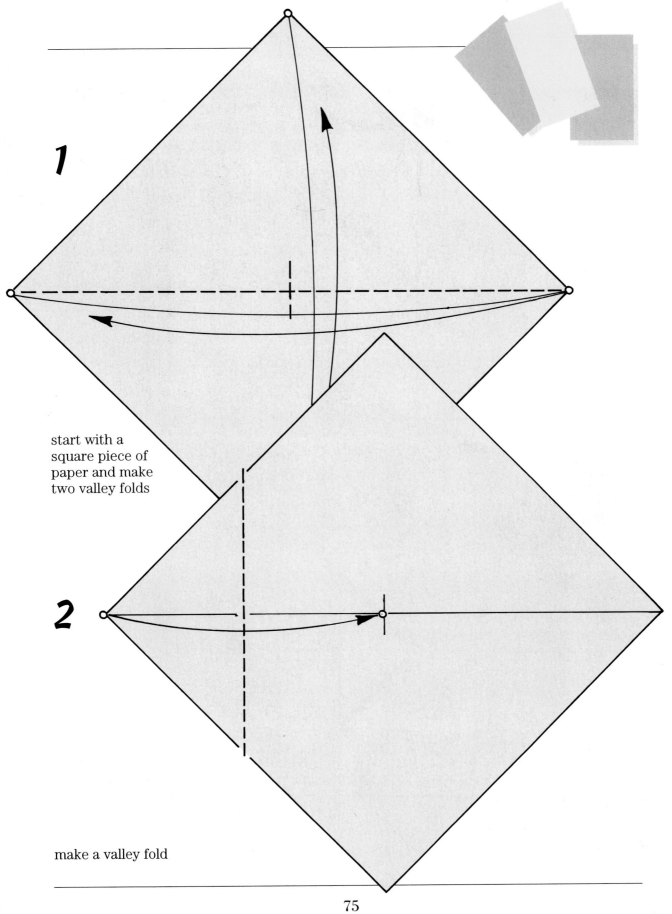

1

start with a
square piece of
paper and make
two valley folds

2

make a valley fold

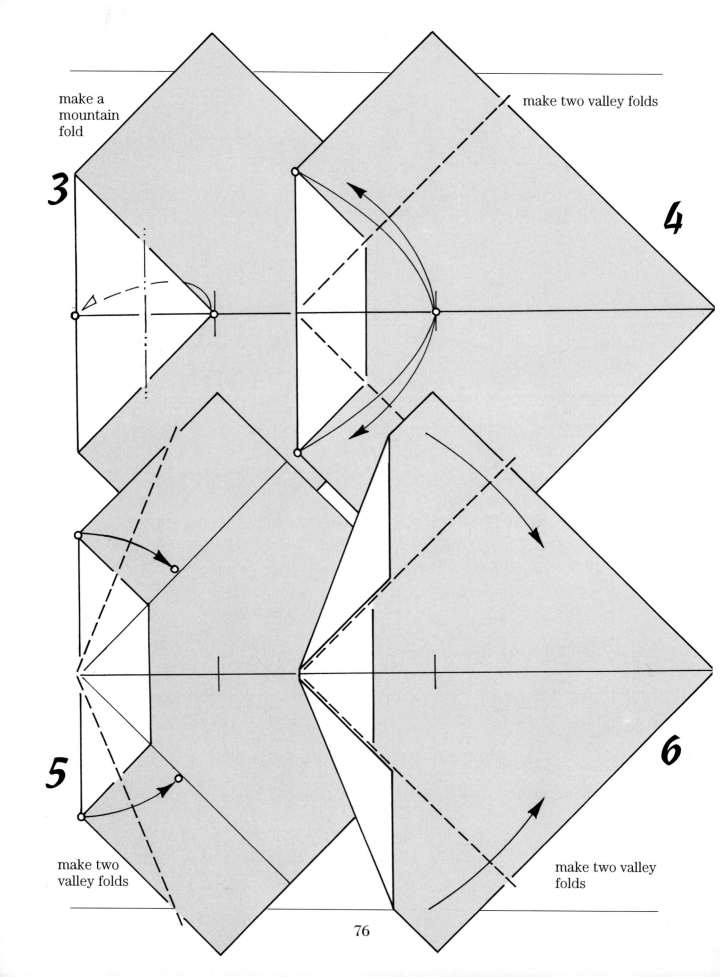

3 make a mountain fold

4 make two valley folds

5 make two valley folds

6 make two valley folds

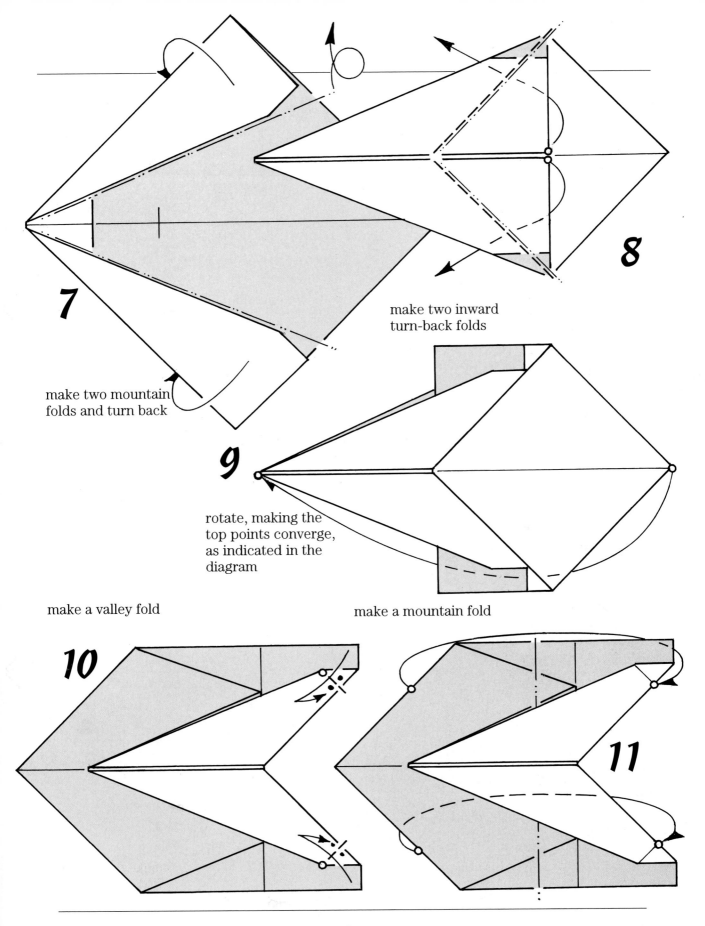

7

make two mountain
folds and turn back

8

make two inward
turn-back folds

9

rotate, making the
top points converge,
as indicated in the
diagram

make a valley fold

make a mountain fold

10

11

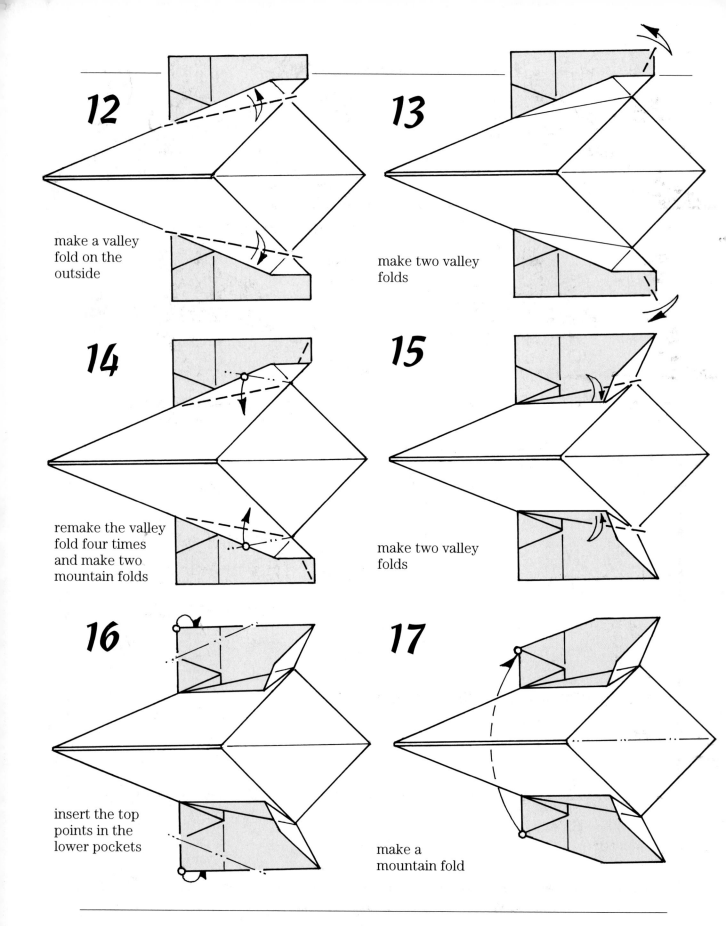

12

make a valley
fold on the
outside

13

make two valley
folds

14

remake the valley
fold four times
and make two
mountain folds

15

make two valley
folds

16

insert the top
points in the
lower pockets

17

make a
mountain fold

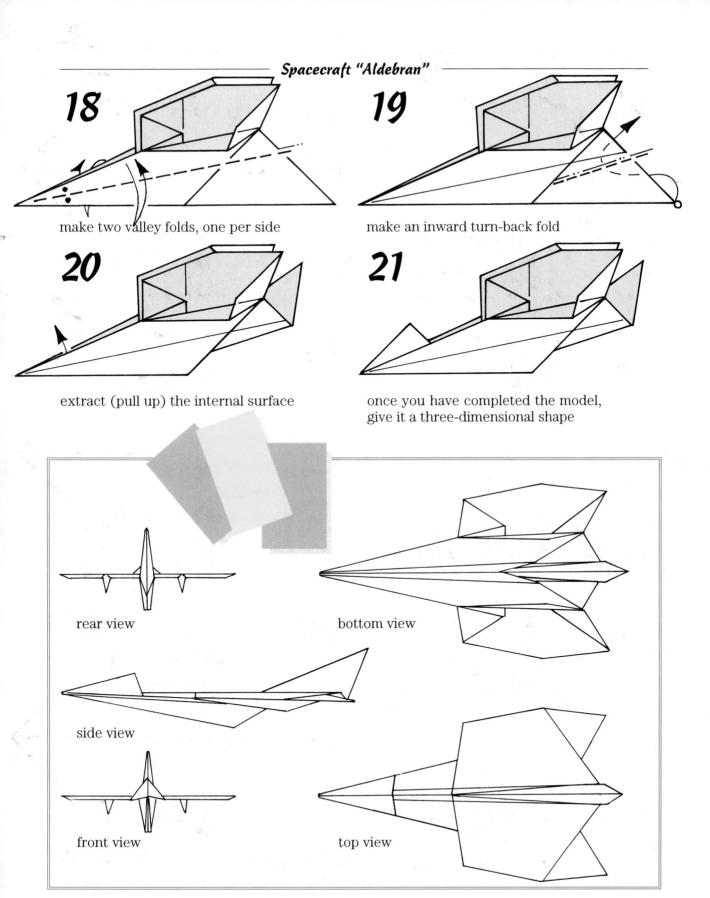

18 make two valley folds, one per side

19 make an inward turn-back fold

20 extract (pull up) the internal surface

21 once you have completed the model, give it a three-dimensional shape

rear view

bottom view

side view

front view

top view

Index